Hodgepodge Logic

BY DOREEN FRICK

ONE WOMAN'S JOURNAL
THROUGH MARRIAGE, MOVES AND MOTHERHOOD

Hodgepodge Logic

Doreen Frick

First Edition published in 1999
Doreen Frick
1482 Sugar Bottom Road
Furlong, PA 18925 USA.

© Doreen Frick, 1999

ISBN 0-9667862-0-3

Library of Congress Catalog Card Number: 98-94787

Printed and bound in the United States of America

Contents

Dedication	5
Hodgepodge Logic	7
Changing Dad's Mind	9
When Sisters Argue	11
Brave Mom	13
You Want Me to Live in a Bus?	15
Evening Rituals	19
Sponge Baths	23
The Little Red Cabin	25
The Waving Farmer and His Wife	29
Sick for Home	33
Wes Gets a Real Job	35
The Secret	39
Mom to the Rescue	43
Moving 101	45
You Ought to be in Pictures	49
The Magic Pacifier	51
Joey Makes His Entrance	53
Ash Mother's Day	55
Peaceful Coexistence	57
The Gift of Love	59
The Smart Farmer	61
The Not-So Funny Farm	63
Life is Tough on the Big Farm	65
The Runaways	69
You'll Survive	71
She By-Passed Earth	73
For Sale	75
Rough Riding	77

Ten Years Later 81
Ten Years Later 83
Jell-O Pies and Stick-Up Notes 85

Where is that Kid?	87
Of Dogs and Men	89
Real Men Do Laundry	91
Phone Tag	93
Drive-Thru Dinner	95
The Caddy	97
The Cycle of Trash	99
Reading Between the Lines	101
Senior Day	103
Wes Survives Family Day	107
How Not to Get Lost	109
In Sickness and in Health	111
Motherhood the First Time Around	113
She Talks Now	115
The Ride, Jessica Frick	116
Of Socks and Mittens	119
A Change of Life	121
This, Too, Shall Pass	123
Constant Change	125

This Book is Dedicated to
WES
Whom I Love

Special thanks go to:

My kids—Jessica, Joshua, Piper and Joey. I really wrote the book for you guys. I hope you enjoy it; I know I really enjoyed having you for kids.

My folks, Salem and Mary Kirban. Thanks, Dad, for pointing me in the right direction, and Mom for telling me to keep writing.

My brother, Dennis and his wife, Eileen Kirban. Without you, this book wouldn't have gotten off the ground. I'm glad I have such talented relatives. Thanks, Eileen, for not letting me spell hodgepodge wrong, and for all the special ideas you helped me incorporate in this book.

My sisters, Diane Buchanan and Dawn Adkins, who helped me move, changed my kids' diapers, cooked meals for me when I had more babies, and most of all, helped me keep my sanity!

My brother, Duane, for making the trip out to Washington with me back in 1976, when we were both young and a little more adventuresome.

My friends, Caroline, Joan, Linda and Chery, who liked my stories, and that made me want to keep on writing.

Dwight Gilmore, our friend and favorite *"dog walker,"* pizza picker-upper, box mover and clean up guy, who did all this and much more so I could stay hunched over a keyboard last summer.

Jim Hutchings, who scanned the book into the computer. Great job Jim—you're the best! Want more Gummy Bears?

Yvonne Reyes of Graphic Design Works for her cover design and kindness. You are too good!

Phyllis and her family at *"The Victorian,"* and Joyce and Judi at *"McHale's Country Deli"* for keeping the coffee warm and *"my seat"* open so I could write.

And to Judy Frick, my sister-in-law, who helped me take that first big step—to quit my day job!

To all the proofreaders who volunteered to help me out—especially Beth Cain and Judy Olson—a great big hug! P.S. Any mistakes that got through are all my fault! I'm sure if Dennis reads the book, he'll try to find some so he can tease me.

And thanks to you—the reader, who just spent their hard-earned dollar to buy my book. I hope you get your money's worth.

Hodgepodge Logic

I used to live in Washington state in an old school bus with my husband and two toddlers. After we moved out of the bus, we lived next door to it in a little red cabin in the woods. Our next home was in town and came with indoor facilities. I thought it would be ours for a lot longer than it was. When we moved again into a blue house by a resort my husband began to build us what was to be our *"forever home."*

Located next to an old cemetery, it was the home I had been dreaming of since the day I moved into the bus. By the time we settled in we had added two more children, over forty cows, a horse, some chickens, and more than a few gray hairs to my head.

In the space of eight years we moved five times, with one move on the day Mount St. Helens blew up and covered everything we owned with ash. I had no sooner settled into the house by the cemetery when we moved a sixth time, to a beautiful white mansion with green shutters that was three thousand miles away from the bus, the woods, and the cows. We took all four kids with us, but I gave some serious thought to leaving my husband behind.

I kept a record of my life in a loose-leaf journal. As the kids napped, I would sit at the kitchen table, pour myself a cup of coffee, and write down the day's highlights—or lowlights, depending on my mood at the moment. I drank a lot of coffee back in those days.

Before each move, I made sure I packed my journals in the same box with my coffee mugs, that way they would always be the first to be unpacked at my new residence.

My husband used to tell me, *"What doesn't kill you, will make you stronger."* I think he honestly believed that would cheer me up. Sometimes I wanted to scream, I was getting so strong!

To keep my sanity, I wrote. Some days there wasn't much to report other than the weather or the lack of money, while other days I went on a writing frenzy. Some journals were so depressing I wanted to throw them out so the kids would never accidentally find them and know what was really going on.

Twenty years later, I looked back at the yellowed pages with the perspective that only the present can give to the past. I could see they had some stories to tell of the *"hodgepodge"* that was my life. Along the way I picked up on some valuable *"logic"* and wove it into the pages of this book. My logic is almost as crazy as my life.

But you be the judge, as you find your favorite coffee mug, fill it up and read about my misadventures. The tears have all dried from the pages of my journals, but if you read carefully, threaded into the humor, you might discover where some of them may have fallen.

Dr. Robert A. Cook said, *"God hasn't brought you here to leave you now."* It's a good thing I believed that, although I confess sometimes I used to wonder what God was up to.

One of my all-time favorite truisms came from the lips of my father when I felt my world was falling apart. *"Doreen,"* he said, *"It'll all come out in the wash."*

Think on that for a little while, I've got some packing to do for my next move. This time my husband wants me to live in a camper until he finds the next place we can call *"HOME."*

Changing Dad's Mind

> *Furthermore we have had fathers of our flesh which corrected us, and we gave them reverence: shall we not much rather be in subjection unto the Father of spirits, and live?*
>
> HEBREWS 12:9

As a kid, I never argued with my dad. For one thing, I didn't see enough of him to do this. If he wasn't traveling, he was at the office and when he did get home, it was usually late. But it was never too late for him to sit on the edge of our beds and tell us a story. He was in advertising at the time, so telling stories was right up his alley.

Dad was the kind of father who took us kids to amusement parks and made pancakes after church on Sunday nights. I adored him. One Father's Day, I gave him a card that said I wanted to marry a man just like him.

That sentiment probably flattered him until the day I actually got engaged. Then the dad I never argued with called me into his study. I could feel a lecture coming on.

At first, he tried to reason with me. The ring could not possibly be an engagement ring. I was too young to think about getting married and having children. He thought I should consider it a *"friendship ring."* And besides, he wanted me to go to college and become a writer. Marriage and a family could wait.

I impatiently heard him out, all the while staring down at my brand new diamond chip. I was getting up the courage to tell him what I wanted for my life. When it was my turn to reply, I told him I was not too young to get married. After all, weren't he and Mom young when they got married? To top it all off, I told him I had no intention of going to college or of becoming a writer. *"What would I write about anyway? I haven't even lived yet!"* I argued.

The rest of the conversation is a blur to me now, but to my father's credit, he took it all very well. In the end, we agreed to disagree. I came out of his study a new woman. I'm not sure how Dad came out, because he never brought the subject up again.

The day before my wedding, Dad took me out to lunch. I didn't get any lectures this time, instead I was given two beautiful gifts. One was his full blessing on my marriage, and the other was the keys to a brand new car!

My life turned out just as Dad predicted. I went on to have the children Dad had wanted me to wait until I was older to have. And Dad—he went on to become a writer!

Me holding a photo of my author/father, Salem Kirban.

When Sisters Argue

Pleasant words are as a honeycomb, sweet to the soul, and health to the bones.
PROVERBS 16:24

When I was little, my mom used to tell me she would rather clean the entire house than listen to my sister and me argue. We closed our bedroom door when we fought, but I guess she could still hear us.

Diane and I used to argue about everything. In our teenage years, I was the rebellious one, she the religious, polar opposite one. I was sloppy, she was the perfectionist. The shorter I wore my skirts, the further down her hems came. We constantly found ways to get on each other's nerves. If she wanted the room nice and dark so she could sleep, I would automatically turn on the light. If she was trying to study, I would call my boyfriend from our phone in the room. One big advantage I had was that she could never make me cry. No matter how long and hard she argued, slammed doors, or pouted, I never gave in and let a tear fall.

The arguing we did might have driven my mother crazy, but it served me well in my debating class at school. I loved sitting across from my fellow students and expressing my point of view with clarity and conviction. All my arguments with my sister kept my skills razor sharp.

When the day came for me to move out of my parents' home, my sister enthusiastically helped me pack. As I came back in the house for my last load, I found it all sitting outside my bedroom door in a nice neat pile.

My heart felt heavy all the way back to my new apartment. I knew Diane was glad to finally be rid of me, and I regretted making her feel that way. As I put away the clothes she would never again have to pick up off the floor, I thought about all the times I had made my sister cry. Now it was my turn.

Years later, I was visiting my parents when I became quite ill. So sick in fact, I couldn't drive home to my apartment, and I fell asleep on my old bed in my old room.

When my sister walked in to check on me, I was crying.

She sat down on the bed next to me, scratched my back, and told me she hoped I would feel better soon. Before she left, she whispered a prayer for me.

That tender moment is forever etched in my memory, and I began making more of an effort to rebuild my relationship with her. It was the last time I ever slept in that old bedroom, but the beginning of some new bonds with a sister I had only just begun to know.

Diane, my mom, and me bonding in the kitchen.

Brave Mom

*Be of good courage,
and He shall strengthen your heart,
all ye that hope in the Lord.*
PSALM 31:24

I never considered myself the pioneer type. I don't remember dreaming about settling out in the West, panning for gold, or cooking over an open fire. In fact, I hated camping; too much work.

But one day, this suburban Philadelphia mother found herself parting with almost all her worldly goods and resettling out in the state of Washington. It was going to be a great adventure. Everyday I told my mom how peaceful living out there was going to be and how I couldn't wait to get away from all the pollution of the East. She let me go on and on like I did when I was a kid, all excited over an upcoming trip to the beach.

Each evening after I put our two children to bed, I packed, priced or tossed our belongings. I gave away baby clothes. My sister-in-law offered to store some of my furniture with the hope I would someday return. Like the pioneers of the Old West, my husband told me we could take only what we absolutely needed. We sold the car to help finance the move— the same car which four years earlier had been a wedding gift from my parents. Once again, my mom held her peace.

At my going away party, our daughter prophetically took her first steps. As she delighted the family, I pondered the BIG step I was taking the next day. I knew it was too late to turn back. My brave front held up all the way to the final good-bye.

As I left to begin the great adventure, I turned back to look at my mother. My tears blurred everything but her great big smile. And I knew then, it was Mom who was the really brave one.

Mom and I love going to the ocean.

*Our actions are like a stone thrown into the river.
The impact of their effects ripple on and on.*

You Want Me to Live in a Bus?

*As cold waters to a thirsty soul,
so is good news from a far country.*
PROVERBS 25:25

The move to northeastern Washington state was a mutual decision we made with the stipulation my husband leave first and build us a place to live. At least that was the deal when I waved good-bye to Wes as he rolled out of Pennsylvania. He left in our old International pickup, hitched to a trailer that carried all our earthly possessions. As he moseyed across the country, the kids and I stayed with my parents and waited.

Finally one August afternoon, the phone call beckoning us to come out and join him was answered. I just assumed when he called, he had finished building the little cabin that was to be our home. With absolutely no questions asked, I caught the next plane out west. I had total faith in my husband's judgment.

When we got off the plane in Spokane, Washington, Wes was there waiting for us. At that moment, I was glad to see him, but that's because I didn't know we were going to be living in a bus. Usually Wes is very big on details. Funny, he never got around to mentioning that one.

If he had, I know I never would have boarded the plane in Philadelphia in the first place. And I wouldn't have invited my younger brother, Duane to come out with me and the kids, ages not quite one and just barely two. When I left my parents' home in August of 1976, all I really knew was that I was in for an adventure. I was 22 years old and about to get the shock of my life.

Wes seemed genuinely happy to see us all, although I'm sure my brother was a bit of a surprise. *(Nothing like last minute changes to keep the marriage interesting.)* When we picked up my suitcases, he seemed a bit anxious about all the boxes I had managed to bring with me. That should have been my first signal there was a problem.

The kids were so excited to see their dad, I failed to notice he wasn't smiling when he pulled over for some ice cream cones. I could tell he wanted to talk about something. I should have asked him what was wrong, but I just assumed whatever it was could wait until we got to the cabin.

I have since learned you can never assume anything with Wes. When we drove up the dirt road that led to the new house, I saw it—an old white school bus. Oh, the cabin he was building was there too, but I could see it wasn't finished. That was the moment I realized there was a definite drawback in assuming too much.

It was all I could do to keep my composure. With the early morning flight and an unexpected delay in Denver, it had already been a very long day. I was not up for a challenge. All I wanted was a hot bath and some privacy. I got an outhouse without a door, next to the school bus that was to be my home.

I had no idea how I was going to set up housekeeping in a bus, and I didn't want to learn. I plopped down on the steps that still had the black tread and watched the sun go down. My mood darkened.

And my poor brother—he was in total disbelief. All he wanted was a lift back to the airport. At that moment I wanted to join him and go home, too. I hadn't bargained on the adventure beginning in a bus.

The kids were the only ones who seemed to thrive in their new environment. It had been a while since they had seen their dad, and unlike me, were thrilled to have him around again. Through the eyes of a little person it must have seemed we were all on a camping trip together.

There was one other bright side to the day. A hot meal arrived with Bob and Sandee Kircher, the people who owned the bus. Sandee took one look at my puffy eyes and quickly offered to come back in the morning and show me how to do the dishes. She could see I wasn't coping well. Women know.

I tried to put the kids to bed, but they were too wound up to sleep. They bounced around on the mattresses in the back of the bus, and tried to get their uncle to give them piggyback rides. Needless to say, he wasn't exactly in the mood.

Too tired to think, I went outside for some air. The whole situation would have been funny if I had brought a better sense of humor along with me. I must have left that back in Pennsylvania, along with my air conditioner, my dishwasher, and my bathroom with a door.

What I really wanted was to call my mom and have her cheer me up, but there wasn't a phone for miles. I didn't want to be the mom or the wife or the sister; I just wanted to be the little kid who could cry on Mom's shoulder. Pioneering was not in my blood. Mom would understand all that.

That night, my husband must have known he was not my favorite person in the whole world. I left him alone with the kids long enough for him to have to settle them in for the night. The mosquitoes forced me inside long before I had finished pouting. Too tired to even argue, I fell asleep and wondered, "Where was home for me now?"

Our first home in Valley, Washington, 1976.

What doesn't kill us makes us stronger.

Evening Rituals

And not only so, but we glory in tribulations also: knowing that tribulation worketh patience;
ROMANS 5:3

I struggled through the first day in the bus on sheer will power. The dishes got done, my brother flew home, and I went to a neighbor's house and took a bath. Everything always looks better after a hot bath.

I began to unpack a few things. Few is the key word here. I was hoping I could live out of my suitcase and just pretend I was staying in a little motel room. A very little motel room.

My husband took me into the town of Valley, and I called my parents. I tried to sound happy as I told them about my living conditions, but I don't think I fooled them. When I got off the phone, I had the feeling Dad was already planning a trip out.

Back home in the bus, I gradually got into some semblance of a routine. We were fortunate; it only rained once or twice while we were living in such close quarters. Many an afternoon the kids and I would walk over to the cabin to see the progress Wes was making. I think he worked faster when we stayed away, but we kept coming over anyway.

Josh, who was the almost one-year-old, was learning to navigate the rough terrain that surrounded the cabin. In other words, he fell down a lot. He liked playing with his father's tools and I found myself wishing he was old enough to help so we could move in sooner.

Older sister Jessica liked riding her toy trike all over the plywood flooring and fighting over the hammer with her brother. I was busy keeping the kids from gouging out each other's eyes with Dad's tools and bandaging skinned knees.

Both kids were deliriously happy and their happiness was catchy. Wes seemed content to just have us all together again. I wasn't sure exactly how to feel.

Days turned into weeks and that sixteen-foot-square cabin looked absolutely huge to me. I couldn't wait to move in. Just like a kid on a long trip, everyday it was the same question,

"Are we there, yet?"

I knew it was up to me to find things to keep my mind occupied during the long evenings without Wes. Bath time was always a good time killer. We bought a round metal tub in town, and every other day Wes hauled in five gallon jugs of water, four at a time. I could barely even lift one jug, but that would change.

Wes dumped all twenty gallons of water into a brand new rubber trash can. For baths, all I had to do was heat up big pots of water on our two-burner hot plate and pour them into the metal tub. I became adept at adding just the right amount of cold water to arrive at a temperature that was very inviting to two dirty little kids.

Baths became our evening ritual and you would be surprised at how much time and energy it consumed. By the time Jessica had washed and dried her doll Susan, and Josh dumped Susan back into the tub, we had spent a good hour or more having fun and getting clean at the same time. I think that poor little doll still has water in her ears.

To wind down, I would pull out a few books and we'd curl up on their mattresses in the back and I'd read to them. There was always time for a snack before bed and prayers and back scratches.

They loved it all and so did I. I guess it was a good thing I enjoyed being with the kids nonstop because in the bus there was no getting away, no doors to close, and no television or phone to distract me.

They had me all to themselves. I think that was what made the bus home for them, and eventually for me, too. I had begun to feel again, and that felt good.

Josh helps build.

*We do not remember days
we remember moments.*
CESARE PAVESE

Sponge Baths

But godliness with contentment is great gain. For we brought nothing into this world, and it is certain we can carry nothing out.
I TIMOTHY 6:6,7

I suppose a bus could be a very nice place to live. I've seen some spacious celebrity tour buses on television where the stars have all the comforts of home, and even many luxuries, all of them on wheels.

A school bus is another story altogether. Even with its seats removed, it couldn't be considered roomy for a family of four. The luxury was a roof over one's head and the opportunity it provided for the people who lived inside to learn to work with and around each other.

Take, for example, sponge baths. Being in such close quarters required some effort be made in the realm of hygiene. With no running water for a toilet or a tub, the only alternative for me one hot August evening, was to try a sponge bath.

I had an idea of how to go about it because I had one in the hospital after I gave birth to Josh. The reason it stuck so clearly in my mind was that it was given on a busy night, when I was unceremoniously left in a small *"holding area"* after delivery. Everyone must have been having a baby that night because they had no empty patient rooms to wheel me to. I was left to pass the time watching my i.v. drip, and wonder where they had put my husband. I assumed he had been whisked away after momentarily bonding with the baby, so I could have my sponge bath in "private."

Not one year later I was in a bus full of curtainless windows with two toddlers not falling asleep in the back, desperately looking for some privacy. While I heated some water, I hung up towels in most of the windows, and sent Wes outside the bus door to stand guard. For added protection, I hunkered down between some boxes, and my first sponge bath in the bus was a huge success.

As sponge baths became a daily ritual, I was always amazed by how little water it actually took to get myself clean.

My mother used to tell me she could never start her day without her morning bath. Once I moved to Washington, the closest I got to stretching out in a body of water was in the wading pool we bought the kids.

Out in the meadow, the sun heated the pool water all morning until it felt like bath water. Each afternoon, the kids and I would walk down the mountain, pick out the grasshoppers that had beaten us into the pool, and jump in.

Pool time was followed by nap time that sometimes began as I carried tired kids up the dusty trail and into the bus. By that time I was ready for another sponge bath.

Wes and I got along unusually well during the time we were living like hippies in a bus. The nights were cozy with the stars and moon shining in all around us. We had campfires and roasted hot dogs and marshmallows. We were living a simple life, like on the *"Little House on the Prairie"* television series. Although Wes didn't play the fiddle each night like Charles Ingalls, he did keep us all in good spirits. I discovered a good sense of humor, and a daily sponge bath, got me through the rough spots.

Almost one-year-old Josh with me in the back of the bus. We actually look happy—I must have recently had a sponge bath.

The Little Red Cabin

*For God hath not given us the spirit of fear;
but of power, and of love, and of a sound mind.*
II TIMOTHY 1:7

It poured the day we were planning to move into the cabin. My husband suggested we relax a little and spend another day in the bus until the weather broke. I hoped he was kidding; how could I relax? I had a severe case of *"bus fever"* and made up my mind I would be moved by day's end, with or without his help.

I calmly dressed the kids in their rain slickers and galoshes, shoved a few bags of clothes and toys in their hands, opened the bus door, and pointed them towards the cabin. Wes started to protest, but when he saw two-year-old Jessica, carrying her baby doll Susan and slopping through the mud, he was shamed into helping us.

Built on the side of a mountain, it was an adorable little cabin. It was painted red with white trim around the windows, and had a deck in the works. It was early September, but already we had cords of firewood stacked underneath the front porch. Unfortunately, the porch had no railing and since it was off the ground, I worried our kids would take a spill before Wes got the railings built. His theory was, don't let them out the front door, and they won't fall. Life is so very simple for men.

Inside, we had a nice loft with a window for Josh to look out of when he was in his crib. Jessica's bed, and all their toys and clothes took up another corner. Wes built a ladder up to the loft with a trap door which, when closed, gave the kids plenty of room to play. But when it was open? Certainly, the cabin wasn't childproof, even if he did bolt a wrought iron fence at the loft's edge.

Wes' idea of fun was to throw a wiffle ball from the downstairs, up to the kids in the loft to see if they could catch it. I hoped skinny little Jessica wouldn't be able to squeeze through the railing, and that Josh the climber, wouldn't go over it. Despite my anxiety, I'm sure they thought this house was better than the playgrounds back home.

Bob and Sandee's kids came over, and while they kept ours

occupied upstairs, I busied myself making the cabin feel like home. This move was not nearly as traumatic as my last one! I was actually singing while I unpacked.

Downstairs, our queen-size bed took up the back corner of the cabin. Next to the bed, on Wes' side, was my flakeboard counter where I set up my kitchen. Wes soon discovered he could roll over in bed, reach into the crock-pot where Josh's bottle was warmed, and toss it up to Jessica to give her little brother. That was when I realized the value of the wiffle ball toss game!

Directly at the foot of our bed was our kitchen table, two adult chairs, one high chair, and a baby butler on wheels for Josh. His seat folded down, and the whole thing could be stored under the kitchen table between meals. This was a great convenience in a house that measured sixteen-feet-square.

We had a fantastic view from the picture window. From the kitchen table we could watch the kids playing in the clearing, see cars driving up the long and winding road that led to our cabin, and gaze at the meadow below. Fortunately, the outhouse was way off to the side of the cabin, and out of view. I also considered it a blessing both kids were still in diapers.

We bought a black wood stove and sat it back in the far corner opposite the kitchen table. The next day we realized it wasn't back far enough; Joshua found it with his forehead. To prevent future mishaps, Wes built a barrier around the stove until we needed to use it later on that year.

Eventually, Wes wanted to add on to the cabin and build a pantry. It didn't take long for the pantry to become a top priority and Josh was also the reason for this. My canned goods were all stored in wooden crates that were turned on their sides, and pushed under my flakeboard counter. One day when I wasn't keeping both eyes on Josh, he entertained himself by removing the labels from all the cans. When that was done, he decorated our floor with pancake syrup. Meals were a little crazy for the next week, but at least I got a pantry.

My kitchen was very compact. I could cook, wash the dishes and put them away, and hardly even have to move. I had a tabletop oven on the counter, along with a two-burner hot plate, a radio, a crock-pot and a dish drainer. My sink was a metal tub on wheels that was stored under the counter when not in use. To conserve water, I only did the dishes once a day, so I hid all the dirty ones in the tub. Slipped under the counter like that fooled me into thinking I never had any dishes to do.

Life in the cabin was life at its simplest. There was very little housework because there was very little house! Laundry was done every Monday when we went to town. Every Monday night, we folded a week's worth of clean clothes while we watched Monday Night Football together. The rest of my time at home was used to get back to basics. But first, I had to learn the basics, which was my next real challenge. Thankfully, my attitude about challenges was rapidly improving. I was beginning to feel like I belonged here.

Doreen, Jessica, Wes and Josh and the little red cabin in Valley, Washington, 1976.

The Waving Farmer and His Wife

But let all those that put their trust in thee rejoice: let them ever shout for joy, because thou defendest them: let them also that love thy name be joyful in thee.

PSALM 5:11

I used to like to go to town because I enjoyed seeing all the farmers out in their fields. One particular farmer and his wife used to wave to us as they rode on their tractor. Where I came from, folks didn't just wave to people they have never met, but it seemed like such a peculiarly nice gesture, I waved back. I sort of hoped we'd run into the farmer and his wife someday when we were in town.

I was becoming so lonely for my family back in Pennsylvania. Sundays were especially rough because we all used to get together and have dinner at my mom and dad's. Once we left Pennsylvania and our families, Sundays were the hardest day of the week for me.

One Sunday evening shortly after we'd moved into the cabin, I made my husband take me to church. We sponge bathed the kids and found some *"Sunday-go-to-meeting clothes,"* and headed into the neighboring town of Chewelah.

We drove up and down the streets, looking for a church. We saw a sign for one and when we found it, discovered they didn't have any Sunday evening services. I was a little disappointed. What did these people do with all their time? I was bored already.

When I was little, Sundays were busy days for our family. Mom ran a tight ship, beginning with Saturday night baths, hot dogs and baked bean dinners with brownies for dessert, and ending with our Sunday outfits being laid out next to our beds.

The next morning Mom and the four younger kids would rush off to Sunday School, while Dad leisurely took his car and headed out for coffee and donuts. Dad would show up in time to sing bass in the choir.

My older brother, Dennis drove to church in his own car, and would usually find the family sitting in the very back pew. We always sat in the same spot, probably because he always fell asleep during the sermon. The rest of us kids sucked on Lifesavers and Raisinettes, and were very good.

After church was over, Mom would rush home to begin Sunday dinner, which was always a real feast at our house. My dad took us kids to visit our grandparents, who lived next to a candy store in Philadelphia. We always came home with gobs of candy, but Mom never seemed to mind.

And she never made us help her with the dishes on Sundays. All she asked of us was that we change into our play clothes, and place our Sunday clothes neatly on our beds—the beds she had made in her spare time, no doubt. That way our Sunday clothes wouldn't wrinkle when we got into them again for the evening service. Now I know why Mom never went to church with us on Sunday evenings. She probably needed the rest!

Evening church was a little less formal, with more singing and shorter preaching. Dad didn't have to stay in the choir loft the entire service like he did in the morning, and it's a good thing, because without Mom there I was in charge of all the kids. When Dad's number was over, he could come down and help me keep order. The chewing gum he bought at the candy store helped keep the little ones occupied.

After church, Dad usually stopped for pizza, or took over kitchen duty and made waffles, or some other fun snack like popcorn and hot chocolate with ice cubes. These were some of the childhood memories that made Sundays such a special day of the week.

But once I moved out to Washington, I didn't have the motivation to start any Sunday traditions with my kids until that fateful night we went church hunting. As we headed home, Wes figured my spirits needed a lift so he took us for ice cream.

The next Sunday, I made sure we all got up in time to go to the Sunday morning service, and we hurried off to town. By the time we got the kids settled in the church nursery, we walked into the sanctuary a bit late. Who should we see up in the front singing a duet, but the waving farmer and his wife.

It was a small church and after the service we ran into them again, because they were also the official *"greeters."* Now why didn't that surprise me. By the time we left the church that day, we had an invitation to their house for Sunday dinner. Then the nice lady in the nursery asked us over for dessert that evening!

Our social life was growing by leaps and bounds, much to my husband's chagrin. His idea of a nice Sunday afternoon was to get out of his coat and tie, and rush home so he could sit in front of the television while I made dinner. He was giving me a look that said, *"I'm not so sure I want to make new friends,"* but I pretended not to see it, and accepted both invitations.

Little did I realize that day was the beginning of a new tradition for us in Washington. Unlike my dear mom who worked the hardest it seemed on Sundays, I was making new friends who did all the cooking. Life was sure different out here.

Jim and Lou Myers, otherwise known as "the waving farmer and his wife."

Sick for Home

*Keep me as the apple of the eye,
hide me under the shadow of thy wings.*
PSALM 17:8

Never in a million years did I actually expect my parents to come out and visit, but I underestimated their love and concern for me. One cool October afternoon as Wes and I pulled up the dirt road, we saw a strange car parked in the meadow. When we slowed down, my mother popped up from behind their rental car, with my dad trailing not too far behind, taking pictures of my shocked face.

I don't think I even waited for Wes to stop the truck before I ran out to greet them, laughing and crying at the same time. We gave them the grand tour of the place, starting with the bus, and ending with the outhouse without a door. Dad brought a room deodorizer, some lime and even flower-print contact paper to decorate the outhouse, but I still think my mom waited to use the facilities until we went into town.

The kids were beside themselves with excitement to see their grandparents again, and to have Mom and Dad sleep up in the loft with them that night. As an added bonus, there were new toys for them in Grandmom's suitcase. It was, as my father likes to say, "*A Grand Reunion.*"

But just as quickly as they breezed in, they were gone early the next morning to catch their plane back to Pennsylvania. I stayed in bed the rest of the day and cried. Poor Wes. Just when I had overcome my first bout with homesickness, it returned with a vengeance. Nothing he could do or say cheered me up.

When I was a kid, I used to get a little homesick when I went to summer camp. Usually Mom and Dad would stay the whole first day, cleaning and disinfecting my room, making up my bed, and helping me unpack. By the time they left, I would always feel a little lonely for them. Wes thinks I was a little pampered as a child.

But as an adult, the depression that accompanied my parents' leaving that day was an entirely different type of homesickness. It was something I didn't think would ever go away, because in a sense, I was still torn between my two homes. To add to my misery, it seemed as though this separation would be permanent, there would be no going home at the end of *"camp."* For me camp was now home.

My parents surprise us and visit.

Wes Gets a Real Job

*I sought the Lord, and He heard me,
and delivered me from all my fears.*
PSALM 34:4

Winter settled in and it was time for Wes to find a real job. He knew it and so did I. Besides being down to our last bit of savings, he had run out of things to build. Our deck was complete and so was the pantry. He built a stone fireplace outside the cabin for campfires, as well as a log barn for our beef cattle. We didn't actually have any beef cattle, but that didn't matter.

We almost lost Wes when he built the barn because one of the walls fell in on him. After he and Bob finished nailing the logs together to form a solid wall, they were surprised to find they couldn't stand it upright for long. As the wall began to fall, Wes quickly stepped into the doorway cut into the logs, and they let the whole thing crash around him.

Fortunately I only learned about this near miss after it was over and he had lived to tell about it. After Wes fell asleep that night, I thought about what might have been and a shiver went down my spine. I figured he'd better go out and get a real job before he killed himself doing home improvements.

Our first farm animal was a gift from the waving farmer and his wife, who had become our good friends. Jim and Lou Myers had no use for all the baby bulls that were born on their dairy farm and usually sold them at the auction in Deer Park. I was to learn that in the world of dairy farmers, it's the heifers that are the more valuable livestock. They eventually grow up and become the milk producers.

Baby bulls just grow up and become a problem. All it takes is one healthy bull to *"take care"* of a small herd of cows, if you know what I mean. That's the cold hard facts of life, the birds and the bees, and all I wanted to know about that delicate subject!

Wes saw an opportunity for some cheap hamburgers and steaks down the road, and happily took one of the baby bulls off their hands. Our kids couldn't wait for him to bring home the new pet.

They decided to name him *Brown Bull*. As soon as Wes

unloaded Brown Bull from the back of his truck, they wanted to help feed him. They were surprised at how quickly he gobbled down his bottle of milk replacer.

The next morning they were even more surprised to learn that the calf got fed before they did. As Wes prepared the calf's bottle, I could hear Jess and Josh begin to protest—they wanted their cereal and milk first. But they obediently trudged out the back door and followed their dad out to feed the calf who was bellowing for his morning bottle.

This time the calf was too much for the kids to bottle feed alone. He was so hungry he yanked the bottle right out of their hands. In just a few gulps the milk was gone, and Jessica wanted to go back to the cabin and make him another. Wes had her feed him some grain instead, while Josh helped shovel out the wet sawdust, and put down fresh bedding. I think my kids thought this kind of work was really fun.

As Brown Bull thrived in his new environment, Wes decided to double the herd by adding another calf who appropriately was named *A Meal*. It was time to tell the kids that these were not pets. Wes figured what we needed to get them was a real pet, and brought home a puppy we named *AJ*.

Christmas was almost upon us, and we still didn't have a clue about what to do for money. We were eating a lot more peanut butter and jelly sandwiches on homemade bread and rationing our trips to town.

Heading home one afternoon, Wes saw a store for sale. After a quick call to my father, we were in the Christian bookstore business. It was small, but it was a start. Once in a while Wes even took the kids to work with him and they helped build shelving and clean the floors. I think they still thought work was fun.

Things were slow at first, but it was the only store of its kind in a forty-five mile radius and it caught on. Wes was doing a nice job as a shopkeeper, but I wondered how long it would be until he was bored.

Wes was never the kind of guy who liked to stay too long in one place, after all, wasn't that how we ended up out in Washington? I was fairly sure the bookstore wouldn't hold his interest long, so it came as no surprise when after about six months into the project, he was talking about pursuing another occupation. I had already lost track of exactly how many different jobs he'd had since I'd met him.

Wes and I met at a church in Fort Washington, Pennsylvania, when I was sixteen. Four years older than I, he was working nights as a baker for Bob's father. Shortly after our courtship and marriage, the bakery was sold and he was out of a job. Wes decided to try the life insurance business. It didn't take him long to find out he hated it.

He had a factory job for a little while, then he built swimming pools, and paved driveways, and somewhere in between, he fathered our two children, and changed jobs again. This time he decided he wanted to build houses.

He put an ad in the local paper that said he wanted to learn the construction business and got a job the first day the ad ran. Two years later, my dad hired him to build an addition to my parents' house. Now that's faith. And pressure. But Wes seemed to work best under pressure, even though the job took a little longer and a lot more money than he estimated it would. In a nutshell, that has pretty much been the story of our married life.

When we moved to Washington and Wes settled in as a shopkeeper, I felt everything was perfect. I wanted to freeze that moment because I knew, of course, that it couldn't last.

There were some serious changes in the wind, beginning with another move. This time I was going to be leaving the little red cabin in the woods, and moving into a slightly bigger white house in the town where we had the bookstore.

You would have thought the idea of moving back into civilization with running water and a phone, a place where we didn't have to chop wood to warm us or drive up a long dirt road filled with ruts to get to our door, would have made me extremely happy. To my surprise, I felt I was saying good-bye forever to my newly found peaceful life.

Things seemed to be happening to me either too fast or too slow, and all I wanted was to be in that magical place somewhere in between.

The Secret

*Like as a father pitieth his children,
so the Lord pitieth them that fear Him.
For He knoweth our frame;
He remembereth that we are dust.*

PSALM 103:13,14

The year we lived in town was very productive. We started a second business and I got pregnant. Why I got pregnant at such an inconvenient time was a secret I thought I would carry with me to the grave. But I am very bad at keeping secrets. I finally broke down and told my husband the truth, but I waited until the ill-timed child was nearing her graduation from high school. I figured by then he wouldn't divorce me over it.

It all began with the move into the white two-bedroom house we rented in the town of Chewelah. It was about five or six blocks from our bookstore, and was a fixer upper. We fixed her up in exchange for the rent each month. Wes began repairing the bathroom since running water and toilets were still very much a novelty to our children.

Everything was going along smoothly at the bookstore; we were making enough money to pay our bills and life was looking pretty good. We had been in Washington less than a year and already we were a typical American family with two children, two vehicles, and a little house we hoped to buy someday.

Wes had begun to show a real interest in the waving farmer's way of life. Each time we visited Jim and Lou's farm he would hang out in the barn and help with the chores. One afternoon Jim told Wes about a herd of dairy cows that were going up for sale because their owner was recovering from a heart attack. After a few late-night chats with the owner, Wes was in the dairy business. For a guy who never even owned a pet as a child, this was a pretty risky venture, or adventure, depending upon how you look at it.

That whole year is a blur to me because I quit keeping my journal. Maybe I was too busy. Or too tired. Or because I had a big secret.

While Wes was moving his new herd into an empty dairy

barn down the street from Jim, I was learning the ropes of the bookstore he'd just handed over to me. I took the kids to work with me and tried to make a go of it. While Wes immediately took to his new occupation, I was having a little trouble adjusting to mine.

Some days I would close the store early, fix the kids a quick dinner, and drive to the barn to visit Wes and his cows. He always let the kids feed the grain while he milked and called each cow by name. He had cows with names like *Chipmunk* and *Grub*, and a particularly ornery one who always kicked him named *Amelia*.

By the end of the summer of 1977, I was beginning to feel the bookstore was a little more responsibility than I wanted. I had overstocked and was falling behind in my bills, but I didn't want to burden Wes with those little details. After all, he was starting in a new business, too.

When the creditors began to call and I started losing sleep and weight, I broke down and told Wes how the bookstore he had left me in the black had quickly gotten into the red. Instead of selling the store like I had hoped, he sold a cow to get me back on my feet. A few months later, I was back in the same position, and my problem-solving husband sold another cow and got me a loan. He just wasn't getting it.

One night as I was mopping the kitchen floor after the pipes under my sink broke, I hatched a plan. I decided talking to him wasn't working. Either I was too proud and he was too tired, or I was too tired and he was too busy. Realistically, I knew he couldn't keep selling cows to keep the bookstore going. It was time to make my move.

So, I did what any sensible person in dire financial and emotional straits does—I threw away my birth control pills and prayed for a baby. This was the second risky venture we embarked on that year, but it was only risky because I knew this child was going to be a *big* surprise.

Jessica and Joshua enjoyed indoor plumbing at our next home in Chewelah, Washington.

Joshua at the JJ Bible and Bookstore we owned.

Mom to the Rescue

*I cried unto the Lord with my voice,
and He heard me out of His holy hill.*
PSALM 3:4

The year 1978 began with promise. Things at the bookstore were looking up after a good Christmas in book and Bible sales. We also had a new location. We moved from next door to a bar to the back of a department store in town.

The milk checks were also beginning to grow, which eased our financial burden considerably and made for a happy holiday. We were so busy, we almost forgot to buy the kids a Christmas tree.

As the winter turned to spring, I noticed I was taking naps right along with the kids. I knew what that meant. I began to look for a buyer for the store and finished up the potty training fun with Josh. All that was left to do was prepare Wes for the big news.

My communication skills weren't the best, but I think he heard me the first time. *"You're what?"* he shouted. I repeated myself and no, I wasn't kidding. I don't joke about things like that. And yes, my due date was October 26th.

I thought he would at least give me a hug before he left for the barn that morning, but he left looking a little confused. I figured by the time he got home that night he would be over it, but I think the shock was just too great.

If I thought I was tired chasing kids and running to work before I got pregnant, I hadn't begun to feel the extent of what real weariness was. By summertime my garden was a mess, my grass was full of sticker weeds, and my laundry was backed up. I needed some help. Dad sent Mom out for two glorious weeks.

When Mom arrived, she taught me how to tackle my jobs by working on them a little at a time. The lawn was top priority. Every afternoon after we fed the kids and put them down for a nap, we donned our caps and work gloves and together we dug up the weeds that were taking over the yard. After a week, the lawn was done.

In her spare time she made a daily trek to the laundromat to get me caught up. On Saturday she stockpiled the refrigerator and that night our house lost all power. I scrambled around borrowing refrigerator space from my neighbors until I could get the power company out.

But nothing phased Mom. I watched her as she knelt by her bed each night and said her prayers. When we prayed together at the table, I would peek and see tears in her eyes. I guessed they were coming from a heart that really loved God.

She read to the kids each night while I passed out on the couch. By the time she left, I was all caught up on my sleep and ready to go back to work. It was tough seeing her go, but she promised to come back when the baby arrived. That promise was a big plus to my having another child.

I noticed Wes was warming up to the idea of being a father again. We argued over names and tried to find two we both liked. Trying to pick boy and girl names kept us from fighting over anything really important—like where we were going to live next.

Moving 101

*If it be possible, as much as lieth in you,
live peaceably with all men.*
ROMANS 12:18

We must have fixed up the white house a little too quickly because it was sold before we even thought about saving to buy it. But that didn't discourage Wes. He had the idea we could buy some land near the farm where we had our cows, and someday he would build us a home on it.

As long as it was still in the planning stage, I quickly put in my request for running water and a telephone in my *"someday home."* The more tired I became, the more I began to appreciate these *"luxuries"* I had while living in town!

In the meantime, we found a blue, two-bedroom house to rent. Since school was out in Pennsylvania, my sister Dawn flew out to help me pack. It's a good thing I come from a big family who all like to fly, because we certainly kept the airlines busy that year.

Dawn taught me an unusual packing technique. She took all our clothes out of the closets and while they were still on their hangers, rolled them into huge balls. The balls of clothes were bagged up and thrown into the back of the truck. It was extremely fast and to my surprise, the clothes were virtually unwrinkled when we hung them back up in my next set of closets.

By nightfall she and Wes had us totally moved in while I pretended to help. When he left to milk the cows, Dawn finished assembling the beds so I could jump in mine. I noticed she worked faster if there was music playing, so I made sure the stereo was the first thing we hooked up. It was a hot night and with all the windows open, our neighbors also benefited from Dawn's choice of music. I hoped they, too, were John Denver fans.

It wasn't long before I realized we had moved into a quiet resort community with rules we had already broken, like owning an outside dog. Jess and Josh were heartbroken when we had to give away their dog. Wes promised them we wouldn't stay too long, and when we got our own place he would get them a new puppy. I hoped a new baby would help but that event was still months away.

By summer's end the kids were still begging for a puppy, and Wes' soft heart couldn't bear it anymore. He brought home a little bundle under his shirt we called *Sloan*. She was a quiet, calm little puppy that I hoped would not draw any attention to us as rebels and rule breakers.

I desperately wanted to be a good neighbor, but it didn't take long for my kids to frustrate my efforts. It all began when they failed to learn proper phone etiquette. I have to take most of the blame; I hadn't gotten used to having a party line when the trouble started.

One morning, before I had properly dealt with the phone issue, it was abruptly settled for my kids. I was relaxing in a hot bath when I heard the phone ring. The next sound I heard was my front door bursting open and my neighbor yelling at the kids. I wrapped a towel around me and came out of the bathroom to see her grabbing the phone out of their hands. As she left, she hollered something about being on an important long-distance call.

The shocked look on their little faces said it all, and they never touched the phone again. But just to be safe, I began to lock my front door.

Wes coined the term *"peaceful coexistence"* during those days in the blue house. It seemed like a good motto for us as neighbors. Although I didn't realize its significance at the time, that was to be our motto for the marriage when things got a little rocky later on.

The blue house we lived in by the resort at Waitt's Lake, Washington (summer 1978 to May 1980).

Jessica and Sloan.

*Resolve to be sensitive to the young,
compassionate with the old,
sympathetic with the striving
and tolerant with the weak
for sometime in life
you will have been all these.*
UNKNOWN

You Ought to be in Pictures

*There is no fear in love;
but perfect love casteth out fear.*
I JOHN 4:18a

I never knew a baby could fit in the drawer of a changing table. I had heard of preemies who came home from the hospital in a shoe box, but our baby wasn't born early. In fact, unlike our other children who were late, she was born right on her due date. And for that reason, she didn't have a crib to come home to and almost came into the world without a name.

When I went into labor we were watching a movie. As the credits rolled we both saw the same unusual name pop up on the television screen. It's sad but true, we named our child after an actress in a Steven King flick.

Just as Piper entered the world screaming and right on time, at the last minute we found a buyer for the bookstore. My church family came through with a baby shower, and when Sandee learned Piper was sleeping in the drawer of a changing table, she brought me a crib. I definitely was not up for the "*Mother of the Year*" award.

But never was a child more appreciated. I was home free. I had my life back where I wanted it. The secret was safe, the corner had been turned and there was no looking back. Life was very good.

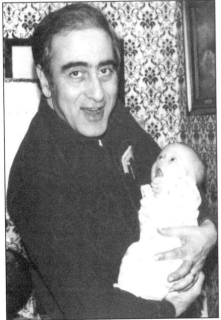

My dad holds Piper, who at two months, already wants to start talking. Christmas 1978.

The Magic Pacifier

And above all things have fervent charity among yourselves: for charity shall cover the multitude of sins.
I PETER 4:8

It's funny how life goes full circle. The lady who bought our bookstore already had a couple of teenagers when she decided she wanted to get into a business of her own. She hadn't owned the store long before she had a *"change-of-life"* pregnancy and once again, the store was up for sale. I didn't volunteer to buy it back.

Not to be outdone, I also got unexpectedly pregnant. It was a surprise even to me and I immediately went to the doctor for verification. I left all three kids with Wes and told him I needed to go food shopping. No sense alarming him unnecessarily.

I didn't think I would be long so I didn't take Piper, who was still nursing at the time. I returned home to find she had cried most of the time I was gone. When I went to her crib to feed her, she was quietly sucking her thumb. She had found a natural pacifier.

Neither of our other kids had sucked their thumbs and I was a little taken back by this. When I questioned Wes about it, he claimed he didn't help her find her thumb and wasn't she smart to have found it all by herself.

I wondered if he was up for another discovery of sorts, but he looked so weary I waited. In our marriage, timing was everything.

Later that week, he brought us to the barn to check on a cow who was due to give birth. The poor thing had been trying most of the afternoon and had a pitiful look in her big brown eyes. Wes decided it was time to help her out. I covered my eyes so I wouldn't pass out when he went in there and pulled the calf. It was a technique I hoped would not be necessary if I ever became overdue and tired from pushing.

Cows must really be tough. My stomach was still in knots after seeing what little I could watch of the ordeal, but the new mother appeared to be in fine shape. The kids were amazed as they watched her lick her newborn calf as he tried to stand on wobbly little legs.

Once the unsteadiness left my weakened knees and the blood returned to my ashen face, I could fully appreciate the miracle I had just witnessed. I thought about how good Wes was in the delivery room with me when our other kids were born. I realized he was more comfortable with birth and all that came with it than I had ever given him credit for.

Over a cup of coffee in the kitchen, that night I asked him what he was doing in early December. Could he pencil me in for a delivery maybe?

Joey Makes His Entrance

*My voice shalt thou hear in the morning,
O Lord; in the morning will I direct my prayer unto thee,
and will look up.*
PSALM 5:3

Wes couldn't believe his good fortune—another baby on the way and just in time for Christmas. He scratched his head and wondered how one man could get so lucky. The new tractor he had been saving for would have to wait, he guessed, until after he could finish paying the hospital bill we had for Piper.

To save money, we considered having the baby at home. When I mentioned it to my folks, my mother wasn't too crazy about that idea, so we kicked around another plan. Maybe when I started to go into labor, we could hop in the car and drive over the border to Canada. We thought they had some sort of program that covered all kinds of medical bills.

The only trouble with the Canada idea was, if the weather in December didn't cooperate, I might not make it over the border in time. Instead of the baby having dual citizenship, he would have the distinct honor of being born in the back seat of our Suburban.

We sat up nights worrying about how we would handle the added expenses. The deeper Wes had to dig for a smile, the more I admired him. He was still hanging in there with me.

Spring and summer passed and I began to notice he had a few more lines in his forehead. They weren't laugh lines and they weren't exactly wrinkles, actually I thought they looked more like scowl lines. He must have had a lot more on his mind than just me and my growing belly.

One night he presented his latest scheme. He would sell the cows, take some time off and use the money and time to begin building our *"forever home."* We would be outgrowing the one we were in very soon. It all looked fine and good on paper. Fortunately our optimism was one of our greatest assets.

Working alone, progress on our new house was slow. Slow was also the key word for my pregnancy. When my due date of December third came and went, I began to think I would be carrying the child until we had enough money to pay for the baby in cash. That could be years.

To make ends meet while he built our house, Wes took a job milking cows for someone else. It seemed strange to see him going off to work in the morning to milk cows for another farmer, but the bills were beginning to pile up and I was in no condition to help out.

I finally started to feel some contractions on December fourteenth and Wes stayed up all night with me in the hospital waiting for something more to happen. The next day dawned bright and cold, and with the sunlight my labor abruptly shut down. I guessed the baby wasn't going to be coming for a while, so I sent Wes to work. After all, the cows had to be milked.

Shortly after he left, I went into labor and Joey entered the world while Wes was gone. I thought about calling him from my hospital bed to tell him the baby was coming, but I was a bit preoccupied.

When Wes got back to the hospital he was a little peeved at me for having the baby without him. He wondered how he could be sure Joey was ours. I put on my robe and we walked down the hall to the nursery where he saw the one and only baby there—if you could consider that bruiser a baby. Weighing in at nine pounds, twelve and a half ounces, his shoulders were already padded for football. That's what being twelve days late does, I guess.

Wes couldn't wait to hold the kid. I told him I'd let him if he'd sneak me in a slice or two of pizza and a bag of cookies. He was feeling so good about fatherhood, he didn't even flinch when I told him I was going to stay an extra day to recuperate. What a difference a day makes, or in Joey's case—twelve!

Ash Mother's Day

*God is our refuge and strength, a very present help in trouble.
Therefore will not we fear, though the earth be removed,
and though the mountains be carried into the midst of the sea;*
PSALM 46:1,2

On Mother's Day 1980, Mount St. Helens blew up. Some 250 miles away my husband also lost his top. And it all began over a pile of old records.

We were moving out of the blue house and back into the little red cabin for the summer to save on rent. The house Wes was building wasn't ready and money was tight, and so our saga continued. It was going to be another adventure, all six of us in the sixteen-foot-square cabin that once housed four. I had a feeling I wouldn't be seeing a whole lot of Wes once we were all moved in. But on this particular day, I felt I had seen enough of him to last me a long while.

Our friends all gathered after church to help us move. It was a sunny afternoon and they had each taken a load out of the blue house, while Wes and I finished up inside. When he checked the crawl space above the kids' room, I heard a horrific yell.

All I could decipher was he had found his old record albums up there. As he sent them crashing down, I figured out what the problem was. They had melted around the slats on the floor and were worthless. It was then I confessed my sister and I had put them up there when we moved in, and never realized the heat would curl them. Oh well.

I never heard such a racket made over some old Bob Dylan albums. I wasn't exactly thrilled about losing my old Beatles records either, but I had more pressing losses on my mind. I was beginning to feel like a gypsy we were moving around so much. What possible difference could a few records make?

He was still steamed when we caught up with our buddies who were unloading our things at the red cabin. As we glared at one another, I saw a darkness roll in as the daylight disappeared. Even as mad as Wes was, he had to stop and take notice.

Our friends all poured out of the cabin, and we wondered

aloud whether this was the Rapture, or the end of the world. We weren't sure which as we stared at the blackening sun. Sandee ran inside to turn on her television. We soon discovered Mount St. Helens had blown up earlier that day. I don't think any of us thought we would be affected by the volcano.

Everyone scattered to get home to close windows and bring their livestock in, as ash settled all around us. It was a ghostly gray color, fine as silt and it quickly covered all my newly moved belongings still sitting outside the cabin.

For the next two days I cleaned ash off tables and floors and out of kids' shoes, and never even thought about saving some to show the kids when they were older.

I also never thought about baby Joey. He was staying with a friend for moving day, but when the volcano blew up we were all placed under a State of Emergency. No one was allowed on the roads.

When the emergency was lifted and we went to get him, I learned he cried most of the second day. My girlfriend ran out of the milk I'd sent over with Joey and all she had to offer him was fresh goat's milk from their farm. He refused to drink it.

I guess he was a bit stubborn, a trait he must have inherited from his father, who to this day has not let me forget those curled record albums. I wonder why he can't remember how much I hate moving.

Joey is happy to see me again.

Peaceful Coexistence

And be ye kind one to another, tenderhearted, forgiving one another, even as God for Christ's sake hath forgiven you.
EPHESIANS 4:32

Peaceful coexistence is a good motto for neighbors to live by, but Wes and I weren't neighbors. At this point, we were barely friends. We had turned a corner in our marriage, beyond the seven-year itch, but too early for a mid-life crisis.

Peaceful coexistence meant things weren't going well and I had to buck up and bear it. After weathering a few turbulent storms, we were both a little seasick. All we had going for us was faith in God. That must have given one of us the determination to make it through the dry spell.

Some weeks I was the determined one. When I would get weary and be tempted to think stupid thoughts like, *"If I just had $100 I would leave this marriage,"* Wes would come through and salvage what love was left. It was a strange season of life to be sure, and one I would never like to repeat.

Our summer stint in the cabin stretched into fall. Sloan gave birth and our little home was humming with the squeals of children and puppies. Wes must have missed having his own herd of cows because he bought Jim and Lou's. The waving farmer wanted to go into the ministry.

Our friends organized a building party and helped nail down the plywood flooring at our house. I was getting excited because it was going to be a grand home—two stories with three bedrooms and plenty of room for the kids to play. Soon we'd be just down the road from the barn Wes rented for his cows. Moving day was slated for the day before Christmas.

As our new home neared completion, things began to look a little brighter in our home life, too. I began to believe, as my dad used to say, *"It'll all come out in the wash."*

Wes building our "forever home" in Valley, Washington, August 1980.

Me and Wes forcing a smile during "peaceful coexistence."

The Gift of Love

When I consider thy heavens, the work of thy fingers,
the moon and the stars, which thou hast ordained;
What is man, that thou art mindful of him?
and the son of man, that thou visitest him?
PSALM 8:3,4

Christmas Eve day I watched all my belongings bounce down the mountain in old cattle trucks en route to my new home in the valley. I supervised as each load was brought into the house and had just begun to unpack when Wes caught his hand on some barbed wire.

It was a big gash. We spent Christmas Eve in the Emergency Room waiting for a doctor to come stitch him up. We returned home to find the move had been completed without us. Our friends and my sister, who had flown in for the holidays, had hung pictures, assembled beds and fed the kids.

The only thing left to do was decorate the tree. Too tired to get around to it, Dawn and I went to bed before Wes got home from milking. Imagine our delight when we came downstairs Christmas Day to find he had trimmed the tree while we slept. He was so proud of himself.

For some reason I don't remember the presents I opened that day. Perhaps I was too busy enjoying the gifts of love I had already been given.

When God puts you on hold—
don't hang up.

The Smart Farmer

Trust in the Lord with all thine heart;
and lean not unto thine own understanding.
In all thy ways acknowledge Him,
and He shall direct thy paths.

PROVERBS 3:5,6

Honest, I didn't mean to kill the calf—dairying just was not in my blood. But let me back up a bit, and give you an overview of farm life as I saw it then, when we were back in the dairy business.

I thought all farmers jumped out of bed before dawn, put on those blue denim overalls, and bellowed for the cows to come into the barn. Then, after the chores were all finished, the good farm wife put a smile on her husband's face with the smell of freshly brewed coffee and breakfast cooking.

So my job, as I saw it, was to kick my farmer husband out of bed, make pancakes and syrup from scratch, and read dairy magazines until he came in from the barn in those sweet smelling overalls. The first morning I put my plan into action, he groggily opened his eyes, and I could tell he was a bit confused. I forgot he was never much of a morning person.

I continued on in my fantasy world by making him give me a real job on the farm. He thought about it for a long while, and finally decided I could bottle feed the calves. I borrowed one of his flannel shirts, pinned my hair back into a bandana, and walked down to the calf stalls in my green barn boots. It seemed like a simple enough task, after all, he had allowed our children to feed the calves at one time or another. This would be a breeze!

Things went along smoothly, I thought, until one day we lost a calf. This did not make my husband happy. He pointed out the goal was to raise replacements for the milking cows so we could be in the dairy business for years to come.

After the third heifer died in as many days, he demoted me to a chore that did not involve livestock. My new job was to hose down the barn floor, while he fed the calves and watched for early warning signs of sickness. The mortality rate plummeted.

Sanitation work kept me out of trouble until the weather began to change and my zest for being at the barn cooled with the falling temperatures.

By the time Halloween arrived, my involvement in dairying consisted of running down to the milkhouse, filling up a gallon jug, and rushing back to the house. Once in a great while I'd sit and talk to my husband while he milked the cows, but he would never let me actually touch them. After all, he reminded me, cows were just adult calves.

Once I let my farmer husband do things his way, I noticed he was much happier, and didn't even mind when breakfast was only a bowl of cereal. And the more sugar he put on it, the sweeter he got!

*The goal in marriage is not to think alike,
but to think together.*

The Not-So Funny Farm

*Are not two sparrows sold for a farthing?
and one of them shall not fall on the ground without your Father.
But the very hairs of your head are all numbered.
Fear ye not therefore, ye are of more value than many sparrows.*
MATTHEW 10:29-31

The next spring, Wes figured we needed some animals on our place. Sloan had been given to a friend after she killed the neighbor's chickens. We invested in some Barred Plymouth Rock hens and one rooster, a Shetland pony, four kittens and replaced Sloan with another dog the kids named *Pongo*.

The kids had real chores each day, hauling in firewood, collecting eggs and feeding the horse and chickens. The rooster didn't take too kindly to their daily entrance into his domain. To fend off his attacks, they ventured into the coop armed with a water hose. I didn't realize farm life could be so perilous.

The fun quickly went out of work when it became a daily chore. But they all did their jobs faithfully, Jess and Josh completing their chores before going off to school.

One job I never gave them wound up costing Pongo his life. Pongo liked to chase cars and bite at tires. I made a mental note to tell Wes and the kids we had to work on his bad habit before someone ran over him.

That evening, I was getting a ride into town with a friend, when she hit Pongo. The kids were all outside and watched in horror. They all struggled with Pongo's death and there was no comforting them. A wise friend told me to let them grieve.

Time heals, but slowly. The husband of the gal who ran over Pongo brought the kids a rabbit. New life was springing from the fertilized eggs hatching under our heat lamp. We began our search for another family dog, and wound up getting two Labs, *Zack and Zeke*. The cycle of life was continuing at the Frick farm.

*Education lessens the number of times
we have to learn from experience.*
BERN WILLIAMS

Joey and Piper make it out of the chicken coop with brown eggs.

Joey, Piper, Josh and Jess with our dog, Zack.

Life is Tough on the Big Farm

*And we know
that all things work together for good
to them that love God...*
ROMANS 8:28a

On one of his many visits out to see us in Washington, my father coined the phrase, *"Life is tough on the big farm!"*

I can still see him hopping out of the rental car with a big bag of dog bones. As our two Labrador retrievers ran to greet and jump up on Dad, he'd intercept them with a handful of tasty treats. He always managed to get into the house without paw prints all over his suit. He was a big hit with our dogs.

He loved collecting the eggs with the kids or sitting around the campfire, burning his hot dogs and marshmallows to a crisp. At the end of the day, he'd tell the kids a bedtime story. To their delight, he'd entertain them with a new adventure each night with make-believe friends named *Alexander and Aloysious.*

The stories were always relevant to what was happening in their little lives and were more captivating than a television show. I think he made up the stories as he went along. Sometimes there was a song and a spiritual lesson in there, too.

He knew life was tough on the little place we lived. I'd write home and tell of a Christmas that had to wait for frozen water troughs to be fixed, or milk checks that were late, or cows that got out or went down with milk fever.

He knew their kittens had run away, that Zack the Lab had gotten too close to a porcupine, and Pongo the puppy was hit in our driveway. In story hour, he took the kids away to an adventureland where there was plenty of suspense and a hero who always saved the day. Sometimes, they were the heroes.

Life might have been tough at times back then, and money was tight, but love was abundant, and story hour was always free.

The kids wait at the front door for Grandpop's arrival.

Piper and Wes feed a calf in 1981.

My sister, Dawn, with Joey at the barn in Valley in 1982. Our heifer, "Zest" is in the foreground and "Kick-it" is the one with her backside to the camera.

Joey chases his kitten.

The Runaways

Cast thy burden upon the Lord, and He shall sustain thee: He shall never suffer the righteous to be moved.
          PSALM 55:22

Once we had two kids who wanted to leave home at the same time. It took me by surprise, because they came up with this idea when they were very young.

It was a summer afternoon, when Jessica spoke up. My husband seemed almost amused by this act of independence and asked her where she wanted to live.

"With Jim and Lou," she replied. "Me, too!" piped her younger brother, Josh.

Since we were already in the car, my husband drove up the road to Jim and Lou's farmhouse. All the while the back seat chatter was killing me.

To my great relief, nobody was home. As we sat in the driveway, the kids became strangely quiet. Suddenly there was a hitch in their plan.

Wes patiently explained the next scenario to them, should we all go home and pack up their suitcases, or should we drop them off now, and bring their things later?

At this point it was all I could do to keep from shouting, *"Have you lost your mind?"* But, as the kids listened to their dad, I thought about how much he loved those two little *"runaways."* And besides, I was not in the frame of mind to play along with this calculated bluff. Instead, I sat and listened and tried not to let them see the tears welling up in my eyes.

It seemed like we sat in the driveway for a long, long time. I just knew Jim and Lou and their four happy-go-lucky teenagers would pull up, and our kids would be gone for good.

And who wouldn't want to live there? Our house must have seemed terribly boring after spending time with them. After all, I even liked being there more than being home!

Thankfully, little kids may be long on ideas, but are short on patience. Ours finally gave up on their imagined *"perfect family"* and decided not to leave home that day.

Sometimes though, I can't help but wonder, what if Jim

and Lou had been home that afternoon?

Josh and Jess, our little runaways.

*Parents can only give good advice
or put children on the right paths,
but the final forming of a person's character
lies in their own hands.*
ANNE FRANK

You'll Survive

*Commit thy way unto the Lord;
trust also in Him;
and He shall bring it to pass.*
PSALM 37:5

I found an old cassette labeled, *"Life in Washington."* As I listened, I heard a much younger sounding me talking to my folks who lived in Pennsylvania. I could almost see myself sitting there at my kitchen table, with the kids playing nearby. In the background, I could hear our daughter Piper, who was three years old at the time. She was mimicking what must have been my catch phrase that year. Over and over her little voice was chirping, *"You'll survive! You'll survive!"*

At the time I recorded the tape, I was laughing, but thinking back on our lives, I think I sound almost unsympathetic.

After all, as I remember it, life was tough back then. I hope I didn't casually say, *"Oh, you'll survive,"* to my husband after the well caved in on him. I remember looking out the window in horror as the backhoe guy pulled him out, minus his boots. Since money was tight, my husband made him dig them out of the clay, too.

This was not our first traumatic experience with a well. When we dug our first well, we ran out of money before we hit water. That meant we had to *"survive"* another year of hauling water until we could afford to try again. After four tries, my survival instincts were beginning to wear thin.

I might have jokingly told my husband he'd survive when I left him with the four kids so I could fly out to Seattle to be in a wedding. While I was away, the kids began to look funny. It's a good thing my husband had the chicken pox as a youngster. I wish I had taken a picture of that crew when I returned. Never was a man so happy to go back to work! Only one child really suffered with them, and come to think of it, she was the three-year-old!

Only once did Wes tell me to save something as a memento of the hard times we'd been through. The milk check was late, we had no money, not even enough to buy a postage stamp. He told me to write that day down, that we were too broke to buy a nineteen-cent stamp. He said one day we would look back at that note and know that *"we survived."*

Now all I want to figure out is why the three-year-old was telling our older children they would survive. I'll have to put the tape back in and listen harder. Oh well, no doubt they survived!

Doing dishes was a breeze once we got running water!

She By-Passed Earth

*But they that wait upon the Lord
shall renew their strength;
they shall mount up with wings as eagles;
they shall run, and not be weary;
and they shall walk, and not faint.*

ISAIAH 40:31

It broke my heart to watch Memorial Day visitors struggle through the overgrown brush in the old cemetery next door. Forest Center Cemetery had a charm to it, and in 1983 we began to clean it up.

In the spring the scent of lilacs and wildflowers beckoned me to walk over and enjoy them. The children would go to the cemetery and pick fresh flowers for my kitchen table. As they noticed the graves of little children buried there, they would place a flower on each headstone.

While Wes was busy with the dairy, drilling a well, and putting on a tin roof, he still made time each week to mow the cemetery. The kids followed him and picked up dead branches fallen from grand old trees.

Some of the folks who visited the cemetery stopped to tell us stories of loved ones buried there: a child, run over by a wagon wheel, babies lost to disease, or young men killed in war. Life was hard, but it didn't seem to harden these old-timers.

When I became pregnant that summer, the kids were the only ones really excited about the news. We were too broke to think about anything but money. I lay awake nights worrying.

In August I went back to Pennsylvania to be in my sister, Diane's wedding. While I was there, I had lots of time to think while being nourished by my mom and her homemade soup. My spirits lifted. When I returned home to Wes, I brought my other sister, Dawn back with me. By this time, Washington was her second home. Dawn said she would stay with us until the baby arrived.

But one week before my due date, our baby died. We laid

Catherine Jordan Frick to rest in the cemetery, next to an old tree. At her burial, my father with tears in his eyes, comforted me with these words, *"She by-passed Earth and went straight to Heaven."*

More tears would fall before I could smile again. Life seemed very cruel. This was not the perfect life I had planned on.

Me at the Forest Center Cemetery in Valley, Washington, before we began the cleanup project later that year, 1983.

Mom cheers me up.

For Sale

*For he looked for a city which hath foundations,
whose builder and maker is God.*
HEBREWS 11:10

There's a song by Hal Ketchum that goes: *"There are certain things in life, that do not go the way we planned them."*

I understand that sentiment exactly. After our fourth Christmas in what I thought was our *"forever home,"* Wes was ready to pack it up and move back to Pennsylvania. After living in Washington for almost eight years, I had finally made it my home. I wanted to stay, and tried to talk him out of the move. He said I could stay if I wanted, but he was moving back. He'd had enough.

In the next six months we sold everything; the cows, the tractor, the Suburban, and the house. Not all to the same person, of course, but it amazed me how quickly it all changed hands. During this time period Dawn had already decided to settle out in Washington, which only made my leaving more difficult. But I had to go. After all Wes and I had been through, I had discovered *"home"* was wherever he was.

I wrote my parents and told them of our plans to come back, and mentioned my feeling a little torn about the decision. I received a letter in reply that eased my mind. Dad quoted some verses from Hebrews 11 that spoke of Abraham leaving his home, trusting God, and being blessed for it. That made me feel better. After all, I wasn't going to a strange land; at age thirty I was going back home.

I began to see that change was inevitable, especially living with Wes. I told the kids to start packing their things, and Piper asked if she could bring her bag of rocks. This time we were renting a truck, so I said she could. Our move east was scheduled for Wes' birthday, Flag Day.

Our family before we left Washington in June of 1984.

It's what you learn after you know it all that counts.

Rough Riding

*Now unto Him that is able to do exceeding abundantly
above all that we ask or think,
according to the power that worketh in us,
unto Him be glory in the church by Christ Jesus
throughout all ages, world without end. Amen.*

EPHESIANS 3:20,21

In June of 1984 we left Washington. The kids flew to Pennsylvania with my folks, Dawn found homes for our two dogs, and Wes and I rented a truck and began loading. With mixed emotions I began the journey east.

Two hours from our starting point, the truck overheated and Wes decided we'd have to do our traveling at night, when it was cooler. We pulled into a hotel in Idaho, swam and ate until the sun went down, and checked out. I liked this idea. It was the first time I had smiled in days.

Our next breakdown happened after we came down the mountain from viewing Mount Rushmore. We almost lost one of our truck's rear wheels due to metal fatigue. That could have been deadly. It turned out to only be time consuming. While the wheel was being repaired, we spent more time at a hotel pool. At this rate, I figured it would take us a solid month to get back to the kids.

The rest of the trip, however, went smoothly and as we pulled into the town of Montrose, Pennsylvania, I knew I was "home." The house we would be living in was huge. I mean huge, like a mansion. We had the use of a mission headquarters until we found a place of our own. The house sat on a corner, about a block from town, and had two driveways with pillars at each end. Inside, it looked as though it had more room than I ever had in all my homes put together. I was in shock. This was more than I could have even thought to ask for.

I couldn't wait to get the kids so they could enjoy all the space, too. What a time they would have sliding down the bannister, roller skating through the kitchen, and playing hide-and-seek from attic to basement.

Everything was more than perfect, except for one thing.

Wes wouldn't be living up there in that grand house with us. Until he could find work locally, he had gone back to his old bakery job, three hours south of Montrose. Wes came home every Sunday afternoon, and stayed until Monday night. That made Sundays the happiest day of the week, and Monday nights the loneliest. But we survived. We hoped it would be temporary, so we made the best of it.

One night after Wes left to drive back to the bakery, I heard the sound of crying from Joey's room. He missed his dad. I began to pray God would change our circumstances so we could all be together as a family again.

After the older kids would leave for school in the morning, I would read my Bible while I sat and drank my coffee. Instead of keeping a journal of the life we were living, I began to jot down prayer requests I had. I realized I had a lot of needs that only God could meet.

Even though I had been a Christian most of my life, I began to look at the whole idea of living like one as a growing process. I decided I wanted to be more like Jesus. But to do that, I'd have to leave the details up to Him.

I can't say life turned around for me that day. I can only point to specific times when He must have reached down and helped me. This was one of those times. I felt I had come to the end of my being able to be *"Mom and Dad"* for the kids. The next Monday night as I watched the taillights from Wes' truck fade into the night, I asked God to bring Wes to Montrose permanently.

After eight months, my prayer to have Wes home was answered and there were no more tearful Monday evening farewells. We were both hired by the mission and had the opportunity to live and work out of their headquarters—the *"Mansion in Montrose."*

Our house was humming with happiness. We quickly adapted to our new jobs and life, with Joey showing the most progress. There was the one afternoon when the babysitter forgot to meet Joey as he got off his kindergarten bus. While Wes and I were out Christmas shopping, the babysitter was frantically running over to our house, to see if Joey was there. To her great relief, she found him calmly sitting at the kitchen table eating a peanut butter and jelly sandwich.

It seemed as though I blinked, and the youngest had suddenly become a young man. How does that happen? In time I realized we had not only survived, but grown as well. For the Frick family back in the East, it was life in the fast lane, full steam ahead.

Me and my mom by the pillars at the "Mansion in Montrose," Pennsylvania, summer 1984.

Joey at the beach the summer we moved back.

Our family together again, summer 1985.

Ten years later...

*Growing old is easy.
The hard part is growing up.*

Ten Years Later

All is not cream that comes from a cow.
YIDDISH PROVERB

It was ten years later, and we were still in the same house in Pennsylvania. As I began to grow some roots, our family grew up. Actually, the kids did all the growing while I tried to keep up.

One thing I discovered is that it's a big leap for kids from elementary to high school. And it's an even bigger jump when a kid gets his driver's license. Miraculously, all four teenage drivers survived, although some of our vehicles weren't as fortunate. In five years, they totalled two cars and hit at least six deer. Joey's theory is the deer come out of the woods to race him when he's out driving. I think teenagers have a gift adults have outgrown—the unique power of observation.

Teenagers also have the knack for pushing all the right buttons that make parents say and do things they often regret. When we were raising our kids, we had our share of arguments—and apologies.

But there was a balance during this season. We had the thrill of many victories, not only in their sports and academic achievements, but also in watching them grow up to become responsible young people.

We shared in the ups and downs of their romances and in the problems they chose to share with us. There were many late and tearful nights. Then, when I needed comforting when Wes had an unexpected surgery, it was my kids who were there for me. Our roles were gradually changing and I was beginning to think of them as friends.

During their teenage years as Wes and I watched our kids make career as well as life choices, I penned *"the rest of the story."* Most of the stories I wrote are on the light-hearted side, but near the end I threw in a couple tear jerkers—just to balance it all out.

Life... like a river... it flows at times like a seemingly endless journey. Life doesn't have to be a destination, but an adventure.
DUANE KIRBAN

Jell-O Pies and Stick-Up Notes

Nothing makes us more productive than the last minute.
ANONYMOUS

I love the little notes I find in the morning. I think those colorful square stick-up notes were a great invention. I never know when my children might leave me one.

I do know if Piper has an urgent request, she will leave the note in my bathroom. After reading one of her notes, my leisurely morning routine generally goes out the window. One morning her note asked if I would please make three strawberry Jell-O pies in time for a pie eating contest at school. My husband said it couldn't be done—they would never solidify in time. That was all I needed to hear to prove I could do it.

Once my kids got older, I developed into a real night owl. My morning usually doesn't begin until about 10 a.m., or when the phone rings. Since most of my friends know I sleep late, the phone doesn't usually ring too early.

As I read her note, my brain began to gel. I figured I had less than two-and-a-half hours to accomplish the feat. Switching into hurry-up mode, I cut my bath, make-up and hair routine time in half. I left the laundry right where it was, and as I rushed out to the store to buy some Jell-O, I hollered hello and good-bye to the dogs. Sorry, no time for a tummy rub or pat on the head this morning.

Hopefully, my husband didn't hear me speed out the driveway without warming up the minivan, but time definitely was not my friend. It was a good thing my friend Caroline called me before ten, or even the quick-set ice cube method wouldn't have saved those Jell-O pies. Thankfully, I had ice. Sometimes my refrigerator is so empty I don't even have that, but that's another story.

As I rushed out of the kitchen with three perfect pies, my eyes caught a glimpse of something on the table that shouldn't have been there. It was the plate of chocolate chip cookies Joey was supposed to take to school for a class fund raiser. I guess he never saw my pale yellow stick-up reminder.

I grabbed the cookies, and made a few mental notes on my way to school. Buy bigger brighter stick-up notes, and start setting the alarm clock on weekdays!

Piper ran hurdles in high school, but her little notes kept me hopping as well.

*Youth is not a time of life;
it is a state of mind.*
SAMUEL ULLMAN

Where is that Kid?

*Small children don't let you sleep;
big children don't let you rest.*
YIDDISH PROVERB

One of the big advantages to working out of our home was the opportunity to have the kids work there also. We took a chance and let all of them work for us by doing the mailings for the ministry. The last one to work was Joey, who during his senior year was allowed to leave each day before lunch to come home and stuff envelopes.

Sometimes I would leave Joey a note at the kitchen table that told him where he could meet me for lunch. Wes always used to wonder where his note was, but I enjoyed the time alone with Joey. I knew all too soon he would move away, and I would wish for those *"bonding"* times back.

I am a big one for leaving notes, and tried to encourage my kids to do the same. Joey, being more forgetful than the rest of the bunch, leaves himself notes, but then sometimes forgets to read them. Wes has this same problem, so I think it's hereditary.

One night, soon after Joey had begun driving, I fell asleep before I heard him come home. I woke up with a start, and began the all too familiar routine of worrying about if he'd been in an accident. Then I tried to wake Wes to get him to go out and look for Joey.

The first few times I sent Wes out looking for a kid, he did so willingly. After a few snowstorms dampened his spirits and shortened his nights, he went out a little less enthusiastically. But by the time Joey became a licensed driver, Wes just rolled over and pretended not to hear me.

I got out of bed and paced the kitchen floor. Then I made some coffee. As it got too late to call around for Joey, I debated on which one of his friend's mothers wouldn't mind me waking them to ask if they'd seen my son.

Finally, I just picked up the phone and called one of Joey's friends. I was surprised to hear the sleepy voice on the other end tell me he thought Joey was home in bed.

I hung up and thought about it for a minute. Then I ran

upstairs to Joey's room, and there he was—sound asleep. Why I didn't remember he would forget to wake me and tell me he was home is one of the great mysteries of my life.

I went back to bed and nudged Wes, who I knew was not sleeping, and told him not to worry, I had it all under control. And next time, I'll check the bed first.

Jessica with her "little brother" Joey on a trip to Florida, August 1998.

Blessed are they who can laugh at themselves, for they shall never cease to be amused.

Of Dogs and Men

*Try to reason about love,
and you will lose your reason.*
FRENCH PROVERB

The dog was wagging his tail, but his master was not smiling. I was late. Very late. The two of them had been waiting for me in the truck a full forty-five minutes.

It wasn't the hairdresser's fault I was so late. I had forgotten to factor in hair color, chit chat and interruptions into my estimated time of beauty arrival. As I paid the hairdresser, I took one last look in the mirror. The gray was all gone, I was now mahogany. The bounce was back in my hair and in my step. I thought surely my husband would notice all the improvements I'd made in just three short hours.

I opened the door of the truck, and the dog smothered me with kisses. Strange, my husband wasn't following his lead. I gave him my, *"Oh, were you waiting for me long?"* innocent look. Nothing.

I smiled and moved closer so he could get a good long whiff of my sultry hair mousse. The only reaction I got was a sneeze. I guess the peroxide was still a little overwhelming.

I backed off to regroup and the dog plopped in my lap. That's one of the really nice things about a dog—they have no conception of time. No matter how long you're gone, they're always glad to see you when you get back. Since he was the only one happy to see me, I talked to him all the way home.

Out of the corner of my eye, I could see my husband checking out my new look. So I told the dog, *"Well, Riley, I guess it was a smart move on my part to pass on the manicure today, huh?"* My husband cracked a smile, and then took me out to dinner. I don't know, maybe he wanted to show off my new hairdo. And men say women are hard to understand!

Wes cracks a smile.

*The time to be happy is now.
The place to be happy is here.
The way to be happy is to make others so.*
ROBERT GREEN INGERSOLL

Real Men Do Laundry

What do we live for,
if not to make life less difficult for each other.
GEORGE ELIOT

I was never sure if I should let the word get out that my husband does all the laundry. We live in a small town, and I didn't know how the locals would handle this knowledge.

So, it was very liberating to hear my husband and another fellow trading laundry secrets at a ballgame. They both seemed to revel in their ability to get out stubborn stains. When I realized the other guy's wife didn't seem embarrassed, I decided to go public.

Soon it was fall and football season. My friends were commenting on how clean our son's football pants were. I casually mentioned my husband was the reason for this sudden brightness. It wasn't long before he began getting calls after the games from some of the football moms. They needed his advice on how to get the blood and mud out of their sons' uniforms.

Now all this laundry business began with the football stuff, but to fill the washer, my husband would sneak in a few towels. The reason I know this is because our kids noticed our towels suddenly smelled fresher. I went down to the basement to investigate. He was busy scrubbing stains in the sink next to the washer and didn't hear me.

It was then I discovered he was cheating. He was completely ignoring the directions on the back of the detergent bottle, and he wasn't even measuring the powder he was pouring out of a strange-looking box.

I couldn't watch. I crept back upstairs, and decided to let him have the entire job. After all, he was enjoying himself, and I didn't miss the climb up and down the cellar steps everyday. Besides, who am I to argue with success?

Phone Tag

A good laugh is sunshine in a house.
P. J. BAILEY

No dinner was cooked tonight. Just as I got ready to cook, I got a call and an invitation to go shopping. My kids were shocked at this.

Normally, the dinner hour is almost sacred. I don't answer the phone, and my kids just hate that. They can't understand how I can possibly let the phone ring and not answer it. If it's just the two of us at the table, and the phone rings twenty or thirty times, we know it's more than likely one of our kids calling. They know even Mom can't let it ring that many times without answering.

When our son, Josh moved to Florida, we gave him Wes' 800 number so he could call us from time to time at our expense. The only trouble with that was my husband will stand right next to the phone and let the answering machine kick in before he decides if he wants to talk to the caller.

Josh will not talk to machines, so if he gets his father's, he hangs up and calls my number—COLLECT. If I'm not making or eating dinner, I'll answer, and the first words out of his mouth are, *"Why doesn't Dad answer his phone?"* I always tell him his dad is out walking the dogs.

That seems to satisfy him for now. Someday, I'll have to tell him the truth, that his dad screens his calls, even ones from his children. I think Jessica has caught on to this screening process, because she always leaves funny messages accusing Wes of avoiding her.

But for me, if I need a little break at dinnertime, I answer the phone, just in case it's a chance to get out of the house and go shopping with a friend. Who knows, maybe she'll treat me to dinner!

Drive-Thru Dinner

*Variety is the very spice of life,
that gives it all its flavor.*
WILLIAM COWPER

Keeping food in the refrigerator is almost a full-time job, or at least my kids wish I would treat it like one.

I know the pickings are mighty slim on Thursdays. That's the night I clean out the leftovers and serve them up as a kind of hodgepodge meal, which is not a big favorite around here.

When one of my kids opens the fridge and says, *"There's nothing to eat in here,"* I can almost feel the hair stand up on the back of my neck. Aren't eggs and milk considered food? How about bread and butter? O.K., so the deli meat is a little old, and I guess a jar of pickled beets and some carrot sticks aren't much of an appetizer. But with a little imagination, I can usually whip up a meal from the bare bones of the Thursday night refrigerator.

After one of those predictable comments from my children, I threatened to give up cooking altogether. Joey reminds me that in order to quit something, you have to have started it in the first place. Undaunted I go through my list of suggestions of things they can fix to eat. But as I'm talking *(to myself I guess)*, I hear the fridge door slam shut, and the sounds of muttering in the kitchen.

I know what the next sound will be. If it's Joey who is hungry that night, it'll be the buzzing of the electric can opener. In less than two minutes, he'll have his steaming bowl of canned spaghetti set up on his card table in front of the television.

If it's Piper standing next to the empty fridge, I'll hear the crunching of dill pickles on buttered potato rolls. That's a meal?

But bless his heart, if my husband is hungry, he'll use his gift of diplomacy on Thursday nights. First he'll mosey around the kitchen, pretending to be looking for something to eat. Soon I'll hear the jingle of keys as he wanders out the kitchen door, yelling as he leaves, *"Doreen, do you want anything from the drive-thru at McDonald's?"*

Who says I need to cook every Thursday? It's more fun to sit back and see what develops!

Joey and Piper pose in front of our refrigerator in Valley, WA, 1982.

Piper and Joey – fifteen years later (probably after finding real food in the refrigerator!)

The Caddy

*Happiness is found along the way,
not at the end of the road.*

When I was sixteen, I wanted a Corvette in the worst way. My older brother, Dennis, had one and I just loved when he would pick me up from school in it. Instead of dreaming about boys, I was saving my money and wondering when I would have enough to buy my shiny red Corvette.

After working all summer, I pulled out my savings book and sat down at the kitchen table with Mom to talk finances. She worked out all the figures for me, and gave me the bad news. I could work full time while going to school so I could get my dream car, or I could give my dad what I had saved, and buy his car.

And so it was that in my junior year, I drove the *"tank"* to school. Instead of the sleek, red fiberglass sports car I had set my sights on, I got a gold Cadillac with fairly large tail fins. But it was paid for.

I hadn't been driving long before I had my first accident when I pulled out in front of a neighbor who was rushing to work. As my mom surveyed the damage to the front end of my Caddy, she lovingly told me they could fix the car, but they could never replace me. OK, so it wasn't fast—but it was safe!

Then one day, my brother's beautiful Corvette was stolen from a parking lot. Even though it was eventually recovered, there wasn't much left of his prized possession when he got it back. I'm almost certain I could have left my keys dangling from the ignition of my car, and it wouldn't have walked off.

But I never truly understood how much I liked that old car until I sold it. The first thing I missed was its deep trunk. It could hold everything including the kitchen sink! The first vacation I took after selling my Caddy, I took so much stuff my husband's best friend had to follow us to the beach with the playpen and luggage I couldn't fit in our car.

Since those early days I've always driven very practical vehicles, and with four kids, most of them have been station wagons and minivans. I notice you don't see many wagons on the road anymore, but when we were raising our family, they were practically our only option.

Our brood eventually grew up and learned to drive on one of our trusty wagons. Soon after, though, I would always find them searching through the sports car section of the paper. Then it was me who was sitting down at the kitchen table and explaining the cold hard facts of finances to my teenagers.

My kids love to make fun of me and my Caddy stories, and tell me soon our family will dwindle down to the point where I can finally get the sports car of my teenage dreams.

Funny, though, now I'm leaning towards a Cadillac!

A shot of me with one of our many wagons.

The Cycle of Trash

*Pride in children
is more precious than money.*
YIDDISH PROVERB

Children are a gift from the Lord. I believe that. But I'm feeling a little broke after all these gifts. I think my problem is I used up all my good judgment when my kids were young.

I was a good mother. I read to all four kids. I said their prayers with them at bedtime. I gave them chores so they would learn the value of work. Before they went to school, their beds had to be made, the flag raised, the trash out, and their places at the kitchen table cleared.

When we lived out in Washington, they also had to feed the chickens and collect the eggs, and in the winter, bring in the firewood for the day. We had a mean rooster who always picked on our youngest kid. When he flew up on top of Joey's head and pecked him, we decided the rooster had to go. Chores went along much more smoothly after the rooster's execution, but to this day, Joey wishes he weren't the reason for his demise.

Time marched on and my kids became teenagers. Gradualism crept in, and I started giving allowances. When they argued over their job lists, I would listen. I began losing ground. Now it isn't the ground I miss as much as the money I'm shelling out, but I've become very philosophical about this. I figure now I'm paying for all the eggs the kids collected from hens that pecked at little fingers. Combine that with all the wagon loads of firewood that has long since warmed me, and maybe I got a good deal after all. If I stop to think about all the trash that was dutifully taken out, I know I got my money's worth.

The trash job has been handed down from the oldest to the youngest son. Soon, the cycle of taking out the trash will revert back to my husband, where it all started. I hope he won't expect to get paid, too. With inflation, I won't have anything left!

Jessica (pictured here at about age 8) used to carry in firewood before going to school.

One kind word warms three winter months.
JAPANESE SAYING

Reading Between the Lines

That which is loved is always beautiful.
NORWEGIAN PROVERB

High school English class can be fun—just ask our daughter, Piper. One of her assignments was an oral autobiography. Generally, talking is not a problem for a girl, especially one who as a child, wanted to grow up to be a movie star. This would be her moment in the spotlight. But organizing an entire life on a group of index cards was a bit of a challenge. The night before it was her turn to give the speech, she decided she'd better practice in front of me.

She had me in tears even though I knew all the stories. Sometimes I was laughing so hard, I was crying again. It's a good thing she can talk a mile a minute, because she had a lot of living to fit into her time slot.

She told her class about her first bed—the top drawer of the baby changing table. Not that she remembered it, but I think she enjoyed talking about how poor we were. She dug up old photographs of the bus and the outhouse. That way her classmates could see for themselves she wasn't spinning them a tall tale. She had pictures of the chickens, the cows, and one of her feeding a calf, back in the day when our lives revolved around the dairy.

As I listened, my mind wandered back to those early years. I could see her sleeping through the baby shower given me after she was born, content to let every church lady pass her from lap to lap. I remembered her toddling next door for potty training lessons, and proudly marching home later that same day—mission accomplished.

Then there were the nightmares and stomach aches she had when she began school, memories she's long since forgotten. In elementary school, I watched her slow down in a field day race so her friend would win.

As a preteen, she was the girl with the long, blonde ponytail. I can still see her, armed with the newest mop she begged me to buy after seeing it on an infomercial. I wondered how a kid could get such a kick out of cleaning and cooking gadgets.

Could she really be my child?

But of course, these aren't the stories she told. Instead, she wove a beautiful tale of family life, crazy adventures, and various friendships and goals for her life.

In her speech, she took them back to a family vacation at the beach where she was almost carried away by a strong undertow. Her bad luck around water continued when one night, she almost drowned in a pool after sneaking out of the house to meet some friends.

She remembered in great detail many small happinesses. She also touched on big losses, one being the day her best friend moved away from Montrose. I was a little surprised at the obvious omission of her many accomplishments. I would have guessed most 18-year-olds would focus on things like that.

And so it was on that day I began to understand just what it was that made this daughter who she was. The oral autobiography was a revelation of sorts for this not-so-observant mother. Of course, I did know she no longer wanted to grow up to be an actress, but instead, a housewife and mother.

After she came home from school the next day, I completely forgot to ask what grade she received for her speech. But I guess that really doesn't matter at all, does it?

Piper was maid of honor in Chris and Jessica's wedding.

Senior Day

In a good apple you sometimes find a worm.
YIDDISH PROVERB

I have no one to argue with since my son, Josh moved to Florida. He and I used to argue with each other on a regular basis and I am going through a kind of withdrawal since he's been gone. Like an addict who craves a fix, I find myself calling him up at work just to get him into an argument. I hope his boss doesn't mind.

When he was younger I used to tell him he would make a great lawyer. Anyone who loved to argue as much as he did should be able to make a good living from it. The real kicker for him is that he is in an occupation where he cannot argue with anyone, unless he wants to get fired.

But back in the day when he lived at home, we would have some very lively dinner *"discussions."* Looking back at them I can understand why my food never seemed to digest. The dinner hour would stretch on for hours since neither of us would ever give in and let the other one have the last word. I was too stubborn and he was a teenager, and they know everything.

Sometimes he would follow me over to the sink and we'd continue our verbal battle as I did the dishes. The more involved I was in the cause, the faster the dishes would get done. The noise level could get pretty high, especially when I rattled the pots and pans around in our stainless steel sink. He would compensate by turning up the volume until he was almost shouting at me.

One day he must have felt he was losing ground because not only was he yelling, but he was pointing his finger at me. That tactic got him swatted at with the frying pan I happened to have handy. He never missed a beat. He was too involved, I guess, to let that sidetrack him. I noticed he did move out of arm's length, however.

We remained close in a different sort of way all through his teenage years. I liked the fact that he chose me as the one he argued with the most. It was one sure way to find out how he felt about almost everything.

Unfortunately there was one argument we never had. It started out as a simple statement he made one night after he came home from football practice. I had his dinner waiting for him as was my custom, when out of the blue he announced he did not want me to hug him at his Senior Day game. That's the game when all the parents of all the senior players meet with their sons out on the football field. There is a short ceremony to honor them and I had really been looking forward to the event.

What was I to say? Well, it didn't matter, because he never even gave me a chance to offer a rebuttal. He quickly moved on to a less controversial topic. I tried to steer him back to Senior Day, but with no luck. The subject was definitely closed.

The next night when he came home from practice, there was a surprise *NOT* waiting for him when he came to the table. *NO DINNER.* Ditto the next night. Maybe by the third night he had it figured out that I was a little upset. But if he did, he never brought it up. And neither did I.

Senior Day came and the cold, damp weather matched my mood perfectly. My intent was to stay in the car and have a good cry. The argument we should have had four nights ago was being carried out in my mind, and I was winning this one. But none of that mattered.

In the distance I could hear the band playing and I knew the team would be running onto the field in a matter of minutes. I realized I would be the real loser if I didn't get out of the car, brush away the tears, and join my son.

But how to muster up a smile? I tried to think of something funny as I marched off to the fifty-yard line. Then it came to me. The frying pan incident.

Since that fateful Senior Day, we have made some real progress in the area of communication. In fact, the last time I visited him, it was Josh who hugged me at the airport in front of hundreds of people.

And I noticed we didn't argue much either. I'm wondering if this is what it is like to have children grow up and become adults. It's probably safe to say I can put away the frying pan I have hanging by my sink. Or better yet, maybe I should give it to him as a reminder of the times we bonded in the kitchen when he was just a kid. And besides, his wife may need it someday.

Josh and me long after Senior Day.

Piper, Josh and his wife, Rossemary. (I need to give her my frying pan.)

Wes Survives Family Day

*Happiness is not a destination,
but a journey.*
ANONYMOUS

I need to get Wes a shirt that reads, "*I Survived Family Day.*" It's not that he isn't big on family, but if Wes had his way, he'd stay holed up in his packing room and work all summer long.

One day, I caught him in a weak moment, and he let me plan a day at the lake. Piper packed the lunches as the guys rolled out of bed. They were already complaining about the early start we forced on them when the sky opened. Buckets of rain followed us all sixty miles south to Lake Jean. Wes' spirits were tested further when the transmission started to sound a little funny as we climbed the last mountain to the lake.

I figured *"Family Day"* was totally ruined. But the rain let up, and since we were all starving, we pulled up to a picnic table and started lunch. The lake was nearly deserted except for a few brave souls playing in the sand by the water.

We started to joke about the day's turn of events, and as we polished off lunch and ordered ice cream, the sun began to peek from behind the clouds. We salvaged the day by sunning on the beach, then hiking to a waterfall where Wes used to go as a little kid. I wanted us all to remember this day, so I went to the top of the waterfall and picked up some smooth stones. In my haste, I slipped and as the family watched from below, they thought I had fallen in. Actually, all that fell in the water was a rubber ball I'd brought along for a game of catch. We all watched as it bounced around rocks and over the falls. After I joined my relieved family, I gave them their stones, and we hobbled home in the broken van.

Later that evening, Wes made me promise not to plan another family day for a while. I guess he'd had enough memories to last him for the rest of the summer.

Just the other day, I noticed the stone I gave him was sitting in the cup holder of the van. And underneath it was the bill for the transmission.

How Not to Get Lost

*To know the road ahead
ask those coming back.*
RUSSIAN PROVERB

I wish I had a good sense of direction. It would be so nice not to have to go the long way, the wrong way, or out of my way when we travel. I've also discovered I don't navigate well when my stomach or gas gauge is riding on empty.

Take, for example, my trip to the Philadelphia Zoo when I was sixteen. I was on a date and having a good time, when I realized that the guy I was with changed into a maniac when lost on expressways. He hadn't taken me to eat all day and I watched in silence as he whizzed by all the food exits. The only sound I made came from my stomach. It was growling along with my future husband.

Not long after that disastrous date we again ventured out to Philadelphia. This time our destination was the airport. Fortunately, we got my dad there in time for his departing plane, but shortly after leaving the terminal we made a wrong turn. I figured that out when I saw a shipyard outside my window. We stopped at a gas station and asked for directions out of the city. We wound up going the wrong way down a one-way street. It was hard for me to keep quiet then.

Our honeymoon was another trip to remember. We started off at night, in a cold November rain, with the new bride poring over a tear-stained roadmap. Our first fight as a married couple started when I let my new husband pass our exit. Forty miles later, I let him miss it again. I wondered how long we could stay lost together.

Since those early days, my navigational skills have improved. Plus, we've made adjustments when we travel. For one, we expect to get lost. That way, if we don't we're pleasantly surprised.

We always try to allow extra time for our trips, so when we *do* get lost, and I get hungry, I can drag him to a diner. He has developed an enormous disdain for the sight of stainless steel!

But probably the best adjustment we've made after many

wrong turns together, is this one. When I tell him, *"Honey, I think we should turn left up here,"* he turns right. It works every time!

Wes and Doreen Frick, November 25, 1972. The honeymoon begins and ends when new wife gets new husband lost in New England.

The greater parts of our happiness or misery depends on our dispositions and not on our circumstances.

In Sickness and in Health

*If a man knew where he would fall,
he would spread straw there first.*
FINNISH PROVERB

He looked so cute in his cap and gown as he waved good-bye. It was such a *"Kodak"* moment. But even if I had brought my camera with me, I don't think my husband would have appreciated a photo of him being wheeled into the operating room.

After hours of tests, probing thermometers, and three tries at an i.v., he was getting his appendix removed. I smothered a giggle as I wondered how long Wes would stay in his green hospital garb. I knew if he was at all conscious when the nurses brought him back to the room, he would be looking for his jeans. So I did what any good wife would do. I folded and put them away in his nightstand with his other things.

After a few cups of coffee, I was ready to deal with the determined patient who was coming out of anesthesia. Naturally, the first words out of his mouth were, *"Get me my clothes!"* To appease him, I gave him his socks.

The more alert he became, the more impossible it was to keep him in bed. As he shuffled down the hall dragging his i.v. pole, I could take no more. I went home.

The dogs were happy to see me, and as we took a midnight walk, I said a prayer for Wes. *"Please, Lord, don't let him pass out on one of his treks to the hall bathroom!"*

He came home the next day, sore, but clothed and in his right mind. I kicked into *"nurse mode"* and made him lie down on the sofa while I fixed dinner. Bad idea. *"Flash,"* the newest canine addition to the family, saw his opportunity to get reacquainted and jumped up on Wes as he dozed off. The healing process took a step backward at that point.

But soon, he did heal, and life returned to normal. The only reminder Wes has of his ordeal, besides the scar of course, is his monthly payment to the hospital. Apparently hospital stays have gone up since he first purchased health insurance, and he wasn't totally covered. Kind of like those hospital gowns they make you wear.

I have one lasting memory that comes to mind every time I pass the hospital. It's of Wes, sitting on his bed, all packed up and ready to go home the day after his operation. He'd been waiting for me all morning.

I had been worrying about him all night.

Riley and Flash, our Jack Russell terriers, were happy to have Wes back.

Motherhood the First Time Around

Worry often gives a small thing a big shadow.
SWEDISH PROVERB

I was so scared to have my first baby. I took natural childbirth classes and read books on labor, so that part didn't frighten me. I truly believed I wouldn't feel any pain with my contractions, just a little discomfort. My mom tried to tell me differently, but I thought she must be mistaken. After all, this was the 70's.

The part I worried about was what my life would be like with a baby around. I remember driving to work, and looking over at the empty seat next to me, and wondering what it would be like when there was a little baby staring up at me. Each time I thought about all the responsibility that would soon be in my lap, my heart would start to pound.

After giving birth to Jessica, we stayed about a week with my parents. All I had to do was take care of Jess, Mom did all the rest. Then, the dreaded day came when Wes said it was time to go home to our apartment.

When Wes left for work the next day, I hoped he wouldn't see how nervous I was. I was a wreck until my girlfriend stopped in to see the baby. I let Sally hold Jessica so I could shower, do the dishes and clean the bathroom. When I peeked my head out to see how things were going, I saw Sally was shaking. Like me, she had never held anything that little and helpless before.

Before I realized what had happened inside me, I heard myself tell Sally not to be afraid, Jessica wouldn't break! The rest of the afternoon I spent shopping and showing off my new pride and joy.

It wasn't long before my *"I don't know if I'm ready for motherhood"* fear was changed into the greatest feeling in the whole world. But it was years *(and three kids later)*, before I admitted to my mom she was right about the labor pains—they did hurt! But by then, I had traded in my natural childbirth books for some really good ones on the joys of motherhood. Who knows, maybe I'll even write one myself someday.

She Talks Now

*To turn an obstacle to one's advantage
is a great step towards victory.*
FRENCH PROVERB

Almost every picture I have of Jessica is of her on the phone. My husband marvels at her ability to tie up the phone line. For a girl who didn't talk much as a child, I guess she's making up for it now.

When she comes home for a visit, we talk long into the night. The next day she picks up where we left off. Sometimes, she talks to me after I've nodded off, and I have to wonder if she talks in her sleep. I'll have to ask her husband about that. One thing is for certain, she never runs out of things to talk about.

When she was little, I used to worry Jessica would never learn to talk. She had a congenital birth defect called hemangioma, which caused her lips and face to swell with benign blood tumors. When I asked the doctor why she didn't talk, he told me if my lips were swollen, I wouldn't try to either. I had never looked at it that way.

Jessica persevered, and grew up to tell her own side of the story, which I've included in this chapter. She was asked to write a paper for her English class in college, and this is what she came up with. I'm sure you'll see why she has so much to talk about.

*Every good gift and every perfect gift is from above,
and cometh down from the Father of lights,
with whom is no variableness,
neither shadow of turning.*
JAMES 1:17

THE RIDE
by Jessica Frick

"Jesse, do you want to go for a ride with your old man?" he asked, "We could go out to eat together or something." Do I want to? Why does he think he even has to ask? My dad is my favorite person in the whole world. I'd do anything for him and do just about everything with him. I have been told several times my first word was "Wes," and ever since then I've called him by his real name. Some people say by doing this I don't show him any respect, but I do it because he's my best friend.

As I rushed downstairs to grab my coat, I saw him kiss my mother and whisper something to her. She turned her back to me and said good-bye so quietly it sounded as if she were crying. But my mom cries all the time, when she's sad, happy, scared or laughing, so I didn't think anything of it, and took my seat right next to him. "Where do you want to eat?" he asked softly. "McDonald's, right?"

"Of course, where else is there?" I laughed, leaned against his shoulder, stretched my legs, and accidentally kicked over a suitcase. "What's my hospital bag doing in your truck, Wes?" But I didn't have to hear his answer, I knew where we were really going.

"Why didn't you just tell me I had to go to the hospital again?" I sobbed, feeling like a baby. I always cried whenever I found out I had to go to the hospital. I guess the thought of dying would scare any nine-year-old girl.

"I feel better than I did last night," I added quickly, hoping to change his mind. But he kept his eyes fixed on the road, and avoided my angry tears and questions by singing with the radio. Then without thinking, I yelled at him, "I hate the hospital, I hate my hemangioma, and I hate you!"

He tried to calm me down and started to explain, but I just moved over and stared out the window. I didn't want to hear the same speech again, I knew it by heart now. So, as he went through his lecture, I went through all the same emotions again, like I did every other time before.

First, when I would start to cry, he would look at me sternly and say, "Mental toughness, Jessa, you've got to stay strong to beat this disease." I was born with a birthmark called hemangioma, it affects the blood vessels in my face. They're very thin and burst with even a little pressure, like if I rolled over in the night. I didn't bleed that much every time, but it did scare me. When I was a baby, I only had a few spots around my right eye, but as I grew, so did my birthmark, and eventually covered my entire eye, my lips, and went down my mouth and throat.

My overnight hospital visits were for previously planned operations, where doctors cut out the damaged blood vessels to reduce the blood clots that had formed on my face.

This was a scheduled operation no one wanted to tell me about, because my parents knew I would worry. I was always aware of the danger of my operations, even as a kindergartner, but I wanted to have them so I would look like the other kids at school. Hospital stays weren't only to improve my face, sometimes I had to go on a special drug to keep my throat passages open, and heart medicine for my congestive heart failure.

As we drove to the hospital that day, I couldn't stop crying. I would feel sorry for myself, and blame God for my ugly face. Then Wes would remind me that there were other kids born with hemangioma, too, and that I was a miracle. *"Hon, you're lucky to be alive!"*

At that point, I had felt every single emotion, and never was being lucky one of them. As I glared at the road, I heard him telling me how special I was, because neither of my brothers could handle what I had to go through everyday. Then, for the first time, I broke our routine and looked at him. I saw his eyes were full of tears, and could hear his voice trembling with each word.

Suddenly, I realized how much my hemangioma hurt him, and when I cried, it made it even harder. As I climbed over onto his lap, he cut the lecture short and pulled over to the shoulder of the highway. Even though I was crying again, he didn't tell me to stop, because I wasn't mad, or feeling sorry for myself. I finally understood what he had been going through all these years, and I was crying for his pain.

As he dried my tears on his shirt, he told me some things that weren't part of his speech. Then I apologized for being such a brat, which I never would have admitted to before this ride. And, of course, we still went to McDonald's first, because I hate the hospital's food.

September, 1977 in the little white house in Chewelah, Washington. Jessica and Wes sit and relax on the sofa, while Josh tries to get someone to play!

Twenty years later, Jessica (age 23) ties up the phone line while Riley tries to get someone to play!

Of Socks and Mittens

*If we thanked God for the good things,
there wouldn't be time to weep over the bad.*
YIDDISH PROVERB

It jumped right off the page at me. One sentence, written twenty-two years ago: *"Today, my sweet husband went to town and bought me a pair of socks."*

The notebook diary I kept provided an instant flashback into the early days of our married life. Life was simpler then, and apparently I appreciated the little things. Like socks.

As I read on, I couldn't help but think of all the memories I had stored in my journal. Funny things the kids did, tough times we'd been through, and the new pair of socks were all but forgotten now. Memories that would have been lost were revisited.

On that particular *"sock buying"* day, I wrote about a small kindness, the kindness of my husband. I also noted in my journal the compassion of our oldest child, Jessica, when she was almost three. She shared her mittens when her younger brother lost his in the snow. When they came in from playing outside, I noticed her hands were cold. It was a small thing, like the socks, but how do I explain the tears that fell as I remembered that day?

The yellowed pages read like a classic love story, the kind that grows more precious each time you read it. Little did I realize as I penned those lines how they would help me as I pass through the empty nest season of life.

I laugh when I think about the new socks and the fuss I must have made over them. And I smile when I think of all the good times we had raising our children.

I can't go back and relive those early years, but they can bless me in ways I never thought possible. And I'm still writing in my journal and keeping an eye out for the little kindnesses.

And what about the man who made my day with his cotton blend purchase? Now when he goes to town, I make sure I steer him towards the jewelry counter!

Jess, Wes and Josh in Valley, Washington in early 1977. Wes was probably headed into town to buy me some socks.

*𝒞njoy the little things.
One day you may look back and
realize they were the big things.*

A Change of Life

One must always have old memories and young hopes.
ARSÉNE HOUSSAYE

Life is full of changes. I think I underwent a life change last summer. It happened the day I got my big toe caught in the window of our truck. Let me tell you how something like that can happen.

One sunny afternoon, as my husband barreled down the highway, I decided to dangle my right foot out the window. The wind was whistling through my hair, the radio was blasting, and we were like two kids coming home from the mall.

I began to feel a little chilly, and keeping with the kid theme, I used the toe on my other foot to push the electric window button, and close the window. Forgetting I had my right foot out the window *(is that a sign of old age?)*, I closed the window on my poor, unsuspecting toe. The really sad part of all this was even though my toe was throbbing, it was as if I froze and couldn't stop pushing the up window button. I think the pain must have momentarily short-circuited my brain functions.

Fortunately, my mouth wasn't affected because I let out a blood curdling scream. With that I was instantly unfrozen, and I let off the button. Ah, the relief!

Meanwhile, Wes who was totally unaware of my predicament, was startled by my screaming. I probably almost gave him a heart attack. I would have been in bad shape then, because surely the paramedics would have brushed off my swollen toe to work on reviving him.

But Wes did not keel over or even swerve, instead he calmly pulled off onto the shoulder to see what I was hollering about. How he translated my incoherent babbling can only be chalked up to the experience gathered from the decades we have lived together. Seeing a convenience store down the road, and being the cool, level-headed type, he ran in and got me some ice.

Once we got back on the road, he told me he thought the screams meant I'd been stung by a bee or something worse. Through my tears, I made him promise not to tell anyone what I had just done. As we pulled into the driveway, I dried my tears, and limped into the house.

As the day wore on and the pain subsided, I began giggling uncontrollably. At dinner, I noticed wisecracks popping out of my usually serious lips. Still, I told no one about the toe in the window trick. I was far too sophisticated to do something so incredibly stupid.

As the seasons began to change, I caught myself feeling more exhilarated than usual when we went for walks with the dogs. I began taking longer lunches, more Sunday drives, and even thought about working a little less so I could enjoy life a lot more.

I wondered if the *"swollen toe incident"* had begun a series of changes in my brain chemistry. Not *"The Change,"* mind you. I'm in no hurry for that to begin with its rounds of hot flashes and mood swings and all the rest. But there was a definite *"swing"* in my mood—an upswing. And maybe that day my life did *"flash"* before me, because I began to examine where I was, and where I wanted to be.

My kids like to tease me by telling me I became a comedian when I turned forty. I tell them that was a conscious choice. They wore me down to the point where it was either the comedy club or the mental health clinic. I chose to remain sane.

But getting my toe stuck in the window was anything but a conscious, well-thought out decision. It was instantaneous, as well as painful, and definitely not something I would recommend doing to oneself. But I have to admit the aftereffects have been desirable and most welcome.

I've come to the conclusion that's what life changes are all about, although I'm certain most normal people don't have to almost break a toe to make them!

This, Too, Shall Pass

The sun shines brighter after a shower.
YIDDISH PROVERB

My nest is empty. Joey left for college, and he's the last kid I have. There's no one home to spoil, cook for, or ask to move heavy boxes now but Wes. I tried to move a box without asking for help, but all I managed to move were some joints in my back.

I thought I would handle having all the kids leave better than I did. The truth is, I didn't know I would miss them as much as I do. Wes tells me I'll get over it.

The first weekend Joey was gone, I kept looking out the kitchen window for his car to pull up in the driveway. While walking to the post office, I found myself listening for the sound of his stereo booming down the avenue. My therapy has been to go shopping for goodies to send down to Joey in a *"care package."*

I told my husband I worked myself out of a job and I wasn't ready to retire from mothering, but he was too busy celebrating to come to my pity party. I wish I could be like Wes. Well, no I don't really, that would be a complete personality change. Sometimes, though, when the tears begin to fall, I try to remember that, *"This, too, shall pass."*

When the kids were all underfoot, I used to dream of the day when they would be independent. My dad told me to enjoy the days when the kids were all home because they wouldn't last forever. I didn't believe him. I thought there would always be a kid in diapers, one on the way, and two arguing in the kitchen.

I've come to the conclusion I can't have the perfect life, or keep things from changing. Not too terribly philosophical, I know, but looking back at the last quarter of a century, I had to evaluate it somehow. I've also decided my back isn't strong enough to lift heavy boxes, and that only took me one trip to the chiropractor to figure out!

Constant Change

*Charity... beareth all things, believeth all things,
hopeth all things, endureth all things.*
I CORINTHIANS 13:7

Lately Wes has been talking about moving back to Washington. I started to make a fuss, then decided to leave the subject open. No sense fighting change; it's a losing battle. I'm beginning to think change is the only constant in my life, and maybe that's a good thing.

I've also decided I can learn to be happy anywhere, even if things don't go according to plan. Even if I tried, I couldn't have planned our lives out any better, although I seriously doubt I would have picked the route we wound up taking. It's a good thing I didn't know what was ahead for me when I said, "*I do.*"

Sometimes, I felt marriage was a test I had to take over and over again. Hopefully, one day I'll get all the answers right, or more realistically, I won't keep getting the same questions wrong. Any way you look at it, I'm always learning, so I'm getting an education all along.

Marriage is a leap of faith that rewards the faithful, a proving ground, and always a challenge. Sometimes it's a safe haven, other times it's a raging battlefield. I prefer to keep the conflicts as infrequent as possible.

Motherhood increased my chances to grow. I tell Jessica I made all my mothering mistakes on her since she was the firstborn. Now that she has become a mother herself, I think she understands how this is possible. Fortunately, all my kids are very forgiving.

One of the biggest obstacles in my life has been in trying to live out the *"Love Chapter"* from I Corinthians 13. Reading it through almost leads me to believe love is a mystery we'll never fully understand until we get to heaven.

But love is also like a gift that when given to someone, grows and becomes so much more pure and precious, it doesn't look much like the gift you originally gave.

So who knows what lies ahead for this modern day pioneer wife turned philosopher and her husband who grows no roots?

Stay tuned, I'll keep the journals handy and after I settle in my next home, I'll check back with you!

When one door of happiness closes, another opens; but often we look so long at the closed door that we do not see the one which has been opened for us.
HELEN KELLER

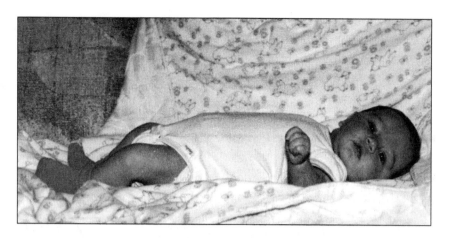

Our first grandchild, Skylar Jordan Handley, born November 21, 1998 to Jessica and Chris. Now Jessica can keep a journal!

*Always look ahead.
There are no regrets in that direction.*